CHAMPIONS OF FREEDOM

The Ludwig von Mises Lecture Series

CHAMPIONS OF FREEDOM
Volume 14

THE PRIVATIZATION REVOLUTION

Joseph S. McNamara, Executive Editor
Lissa Roche, General Editor

The Hillsdale College Press
Hillsdale, Michigan 49242

Hillsdale College Press

Books by the Hillsdale College Press include the *Champions of Freedom* series on economics; *The Christian Vision* series; and other works.

CHAMPIONS OF FREEDOM:
THE PRIVATIZATION REVOLUTION
© 1987 by Hillsdale College Press
Hillsdale, Michigan 49242

Printed in the United States of America

First Printing 1987
Library of Congress Catalog Card Number 83-641096
ISBN 0-916308-88-X

Cover art by Tom Curtis

Contents

Preface

Ludwig von Mises, who died in 1973 at the age of 92, was one of our century's most prominent defenders of human liberty and a dedicated opponent of governmental intervention in the economy. Through his scholarship, writing and teaching, Mises argued powerfully for individual freedom, private property, free markets, and limited government. His theory of economics was based on the supremacy of the individual and the rational, purposeful day-to-day decisions of the individual that constitute the market. His description of the market as a process, set against a background of fluctuating conditions, was a decisive departure from other contemporary economists' "models" of mathematical rigidity.

In nineteen books, including his famous *Human Action* and *The Theory of Money and Credit,* hundreds of articles and countless lectures, Dr. von Mises successfully proved that a free society cannot exist without a free economy. However, he wrote his books at a time when the dominant thinking in economics ran counter to his own theories. On this subject, in his own words, he said:

Occasionally, I entertained the hope that my writings would bear practical fruit and show the way for policy. Constantly I have been looking for evidence of a change in ideology. But I have never allowed myself to be deceived. I have come to realize that my theories explain the degeneration of a great civilization; they do not prevent it. I set out to be a reformer, but only became the historian of decline.

When the history of twentieth-century thought is written, Ludwig von Mises will, in all probability, be recognized as the greatest economist of our age. This may be wishful thinking, but I suspect not. I believe the truth always triumphs. It is always recognized, if only as the economist is so fond of saying, in the long run. Without a doubt, when socialism is dead, when Marx is finally laid to rest, and when Keynesian economics is finally fully discredited, still Mises will live on.

George Roche
President
Hillsdale College

Foreword

According to a study prepared by the U.S. Department of Housing and Urban Development, the current state of repair of the nation's 1.3 billion units of federal public housing is so bad that it will take at least $21.5 billion to repair and modernize.

In the early spring of 1987, Thomas Lewis, director of Detroit's public housing projects, declared that he had found a way to correct the sorry state of affairs in his city's federal housing projects. He proposed tearing down 1,037 units of Detroit's Brewster-Douglass housing project and replacing it with 250 new units. His rationale for wanting to destroy a net 787 housing units in a city already starved for affordable housing for the poor was based on two criteria: The cost of repairing the units most in need of repair exceeded the cost of replacing them with a smaller number of new units; and, because HUD was pressing him to do something about the 37 percent vacancy rate that existed in the city's public housing projects, he believed that it would be easier to fill 250 units than it was to fill 1,037 of them.

Who could argue with Mr. Lewis' logic? The residents of the Brewster-Douglass project could, and did. They invited members of the Detroit City Council to visit the project. Upon inspection, Council member Erma Henderson reported that while she found some units in need of repair, she was amazed and delighted to find that the tenants of the facility had "maintained it beautifully, there's hardly a crack in the place at all."

HUD's pressure on Detroit to do something about rising vacancy rates in Brewster-Douglass and other city housing projects, along with what HUD describes as "deficient housing conditions" resulting from inadequate maintenance, are nothing more than two strands of the same cloth. People want decent housing. They also want some assurance that they can benefit from the investment of personal labor in the housing units they occupy. The problem with America's federal public housing projects is that they lack the one thing which would make it possible for people to acquire and maintain the housing units they occupy: personal property rights in their own living space.

Even as Mr. Lewis was offering his novel solution to Detroit's confrontation with HUD, thousands of abandoned homes within the city were being illegally occupied by so-called "urban homesteaders"—individuals who move into city-owned houses and repair them on the assumption that, sooner or later, the city will have no choice but to allow them to remain and acquire full property rights.

Repair abandoned houses which are not legally one's own? Absolutely! There is now and always has been something almost magical about home ownership which compels people to fix and repair what they believe they can eventually claim as their own. Seeing this happening in Detroit even while the dictates of mindless politics suggest that the way to get rid of "less than perfectly repaired" public housing is to tear it down defies reason. Why not sell public housing units to the people who occupy them? That would be the immediate answer to the problem of what to do about units in disrepair.

But the city of Detroit cannot sell housing project units to those who live in them. These project units, like all the other billion dollar-plus project units around the nation, are the property of the federal government and the federal government has not yet accepted the idea that poor people know how to own property.

The sale, at whatever price the buyer can afford to pay, of all the nation's public housing units to those who currently occupy them is only one example of what has come to be known as "privatization"—the return to the private sector of property and activities currently under the grip of government ownership and control. The papers in this volume, delivered during the Ludwig von Mises Lecture Series at Hillsdale College from April 12 to 13, 1987, address this timely issue not only with respect to public housing in America, but also with respect to the whole range of international opportunities which exist for reducing costs and, as Stuart M. Butler notes in his paper, for "jump-starting a flagging economy" by transferring government functions into the private sector.

Privatization has been under way in Europe and England for years; time enough for evidence to mount that it not only works, but works amazingly well with tangible benefits for everyone, rich, poor, employed or otherwise. But as in so many other areas of economic policy, America lags behind in returning resources to the private sector.

Change has begun to occur only as first one and then another unit of state and local government has consented to privatize such routine services as water supply systems, fire and police departments, and garbage collection. The enormous savings and improved efficiency which has already been realized at the state and local level makes further moves toward privatization at the federal level more attractive. Indeed, the opportunity to save $21.5 billion in future repair costs of $1.3 billion federally owned housing units by selling them to occupants, ought to be, in its own right, irresistible.

But there is indeed resistance. Government bureaucracy harbors its own "special interests" and many people earn their living on the federal payroll by "managing" those activities which governments perform so poorly. Others protest privatization on ideological grounds, preferring the patrimony of the State to the uncertainties of the free market. Because this resistance exists, I commend the scholarly papers contained in this volume to those who want to know more about the opportunities which exist for reform. Let us hope that the "good news" of privatization reaches many more Americans and perhaps they can convince their elected representatives to do the right thing for a change.

Dr. Charles D. Van Eaton
Department of Economics
Hillsdale College

Contributors

John C. Goodman

John C. Goodman is the president of the National Center for Policy Analysis, a Dallas-based think tank founded in 1983. Under his direction, the NCPA produces books and monographs on issues such as health care, Social Security, education, the federal deficit, national defense, and privatization. Dr. Goodman is the author of five books, including *Economics of Public Policy* which is widely used in colleges and universities throughout the country. His latest book, *Privatization,* explores the highly successful attempts to privatize government services in Great Britain. Dr. Goodman earned his Ph.D. in economics from Columbia University and has taught or been involved in research at Columbia, Stanford University, Sarah Lawrence College, Dartmouth College, and Southern Methodist University before joining NCPA.

Stuart M. Butler

Stuart Butler is currently the director of the Roe Institute for Domestic Policy Studies at the Washington, D.C.-based Heritage Foundation A Ph.D. in American economic history from St. Andrews University in Scotland, Dr. Butler also serves as an adjunct fellow of the National Center for Neighborhood Enterprise and co-founder of the Adam Smith Institute in London. He appears often on television programs such as the *MacNeil–Lehrer News Hour,* the *Today Show* and *Crossfire,* and writes as a guest columnist for the *New York Times.* Dr. Butler is the author of nearly fifty articles and eight books on welfare, privatization and philanthropy.

Dick Armey

Often in the news for his forthright conservative views, Congressman Dick Armey, a Republican representing the 26th District in Texas, was recently reelected to a second term. He serves on two key committees—budget, and education and labor—and he also chairs the House Task Force on Privatization. A former university professor and chairman of the economics department at North Texas State University, Mr. Armey has written two textbooks on economic theory: *Price Theory* (1977) and *Introductory Economic Concepts* (1971).

J. Peter Grace

J. Peter Grace is chairman and chief executive officer of W. R. Grace & Co., a New York corporation dealing primarily with chemicals, natural resources and consumer-oriented businesses. Mr. Grace has held his position at W. R. Grace for more than four decades, the longest tenure for a chief executive officer of any major industrial concern. Throughout his career, Mr. Grace has maintained an active role in public affairs. A registered Democrat, he has served as a bipartisan advisor to Presidents Eisenhower, Kennedy and Reagan. His most recent assignment was as head of the President's Private Sector Survey on Cost Control, popularly known as the Grace Commission.

Allan C. Carlson

Allan C. Carlson, president of the Rockford Institute and director of the Institute's Program on the Family in America, has written numerous articles in publications such as *The American Spectator,* the *Detroit News, Modern Age, The Public Interest,* the *Washington Post* and the Rockford Institute's *Persuasion at Work,* as well as its successor, *The Family in America.* Dr. Carlson also testifies frequently before congressional panels and has been a guest on television and radio programs on issues affecting the American family. Granted a Ph.D. in European history from Ohio University in 1978, he has taught at Gettysburg College in Pennsylvania and served as assistant director of the Office of Governmental Affairs for the U.S. Lutheran Council.

George Marotta

George Marotta is a senior research fellow at the Hoover Institution on War, Revolution and Peace at Stanford University. He joined the Institution in 1975 after twenty-six years of foreign affairs service with the federal government, participating in the founding of the Peace Corps and serving on the staff of the National Security Council. From 1967 to 1975, he was a member of the Department of State's Agency for International Development (AID) and in 1968 earned a Meritorious Honor Award for his service during the Viet Cong offensive in Saigon. Mr. Marotta is currently engaged in research on U.S. foreign policy, developing countries, and world trade and finance.

Arthur Shenfield

Arthur Shenfield, British economist and barrister-at-law, frequently visits the United States, where he serves as a visiting scholar at many colleges and universities: the University of Colorado, Clemson University, the Colorado School of Mines, the University of Dallas, the University of California, Rockford College, Temple University, the University of Chicago, and Hillsdale College. From 1971 to 1973, he was director of London's International Institute for Economic Research. Arthur Shenfield's other posts have included: director of the London Industrial Policy Group (1967–69); and economic director of the Confederation of British Industry (1955–67). Professor Shenfield is the author of nine books on taxation, the European Economic Community (EEC), socialism, economics, and modern intellectual trends.

John C. Goodman

A Return to the Private Sector

Privatization has become a new American reality. Among cities and counties, it is no less than a revolution. At the state and federal levels, as politicians scramble to deal with budget cutbacks, it is the newest buzzword.

Privatization—the practice of transferring the assets and activities of government to the private sector—comes on the heels of an across-the-board government belt-tightening. The major impetus behind it is economic: to reduce the strain on tight budgets at a time when voters are resisting higher taxes. Governments that are awash with cash rarely privatize anything.

Never before has the push been stronger to put price tags on public services and then sell them. At the federal level, there is the new Gramm-Rudman-Hollings law, which requires a balanced federal budget by 1991. For fiscal 1987 alone, the law requires $38 billion in cuts. President Reagan and other supporters of privatization have long believed that many services provided by government could be performed more economically and more efficiently by private companies. The most significant American privatization accomplishment so far is the recent sale of Conrail. Other federal activities targeted for privatization are the Federal Housing Administration, Dulles and National Airports in Washington, D.C., power marketing administrations (Bonneville, Alaska, Southeastern, Southwestern and Western), and surplus government property worth an estimated $500 million.

Winning Votes While Trimming Budgets

From a political standpoint, the increased interest in privatization stems from the age-old problem that confronts politicians who seek to reduce government spending: the anger of a voter who has been denied a government service is always greater than the gratitude of a taxpayer whose burden has been lightened. By providing the option of a similar or even superior service from the private sector at a lower cost, privatization allows a lawmaker to satisfy both groups simultaneously.

In another sense privatization seems to be part of our disenchantment with government itself. Voters are demanding new service delivery systems. The entrepreneur, *not* the bureaucrat, is once more the hero of society, and the turn to privatization is part of this turn away from state paternalism.

A Grass-Roots Revolution

The most extensive use of privatization occurs among U.S. cities. Increasingly municipal governments contract with private companies to provide everything from landscaping and vehicle maintenance to dog-catching and garbage collection. Private firms under contract with cities manage cemeteries, museums, parks, tennis courts, swimming pools and civic centers. They also repair streets, fight fires, control traffic, and even manage entire city governments. In fact, there is hardly a single city service not being contracted out to a private firm somewhere in the United States.

For years city administrators have been using private contractors on an ad hoc basis. Now, however, contracting with private firms has become a regular approach. City officials who once thought of privatization as a possible alternative now consider it a necessity. Consider the extent to which cities are now contracting out:

- 35 percent of local governments contract out residential garbage collection; 44 percent contract out commercial garbage collection.
- 42 percent contract out the operation and maintenance of their bus systems.
- 80 percent contract out vehicle towing and storage.
- 35 percent contract out the operation of day-care facilities.
- 30 percent contract out the operation and management of hospitals.

Two developments have spurred the trend: (1) growing demands on city budgets from interest groups which are ever better organized and more skillful at exerting political pressure in pursuit of their interests, and (2) a cutback in subsidies by the federal government. As Washington scales back aid to local governments, pressure mounts on city managers to find more efficient ways to deliver city services.

In virtually every category of city service, privatization is on the upswing, and in some instances the growth rate has been explosive. For example: over the last decade, the use of private firms to manage parks has increased 2,700 percent; for managing recreational facilities there has been a 1,600 percent increase; for data processing a 3,600 percent increase.

Reaping the Savings from Privatization

A wealth of evidence shows that privatization can save governments considerable sums of money. On the average, cities can cut the cost of services in *half* by contracting with private firms. The profit and loss incentives of private companies competing in the marketplace stand out in stark contrast to the lack of incentives and other benefits of competition in a government monopoly.

A second reason privatization cuts costs has to do with economies of scale. For small- to medium-sized cities, the area and population often are not large enough to take advantage of the economies of scale made possible by large government-run services. In these cases, it makes sense to purchase the service from a supplier large enough to serve more than one city. For other types of services, that same city may be too large to achieve maximum efficiency by using only one supplier: costs can be lowered if multiple suppliers do the job. Ironically, the one arrangement *least* likely to be most efficient is the one used by most cities: services provided by one supplier (city government) on the scale set by the size of the city.

Careful studies involving hundreds of communities in the United States and abroad underscore the cost-saving success of privatization. For example, Los Angeles County recently reviewed the cumulative results of its privatization program since 1979. It concluded that 407 separate contracts cost only $92 million, whereas if county agencies had done the same work directly, the cost would have been $143 million—55 percent more.

Studies of municipal services in the Los Angeles area on a case-by-case basis also point to enormous savings: Street construction by city agencies costs 96 percent more than when done by private contractors; street cleaning costs 43 percent more; janitorial services cost 73 percent more; and traffic signal maintenance costs 56 percent more. In each of these cases there was no difference in quality between privately provided services and publicly provided services.

The most scrutinized municipal service is garbage collection. Nine independent, large-scale studies conducted by academic and government agencies in the United States, Canada, West Germany, Japan and Switzerland all concluded that municipal collection is significantly more costly than contract collection—by anywhere from 15 percent to 124 percent. Furthermore, a citizen survey showed greater satisfaction with the service provided by private companies.

Diverse Cities Privatize

A sampling of cities suggests that local governments view privatization as an opportunity to redefine their role. Increasingly they see that government's obligation is not to provide services, but to see that they are provided—at the lowest cost and in the most efficient manner.

In St. Paul, Minnesota, private industry provides sanitation, street paving, snow plowing, sewer maintenance and other services. Says Mayor George Latimer, "It gives local government more flexibility. It gives us options. And remember, we write the specifications. We write the contracts." Here is a brief list of other cities that benefit from privatization:

- New York City pays private industry to provide a wide range of services, from street repair to design services and consulting contracts.
- The city of Newark, New Jersey, pays private industry to provide most sewer cleaning, vehicle maintenance, specialty printing, data processing and street repairing.
- In Phoenix, Arizona, city departments bid against private contractors to provide many city-financed services, including custodial services, trash collection and major street landscaping. Adjacent Scottsdale has been served by a private fire-fighting firm since 1952.
- La Mirada, California (population 40,000) contracts out more than 60 city services and has only 55 employees.
- Houston pays a private company to send out delinquent parking ticket notices.

Privatization Around the Globe

At the time of this writing, international privatization movements are well underway, signalling a bright future for economic reform.

Britain

The leader in the trend toward privatization, Britain has developed the world's most extensive program to privatize state-owned industry. Other European countries, including Belgium, West Germany and France, also are selling off state-owned industries. Japan, Malaysia and Singapore have major privatization programs underway, and there is even a trend toward privatization in the People's Republic of China. However, while other countries continue to experiment with privatization, the British under the leadership of Margaret Thatcher have honed it to a science. The Thatcher government has employed more than two dozen different techniques to achieve public-to-private transfers, and nearly every aspect of British economic life has been changed as a result.

Nationalized industries once accounted for 10 percent of Britain's Gross Domestic Product and one-seventh of total investment in the economy. Since 1979, the government has sold more than $16 billion of stock in nationalized companies, and 13 major companies, representing 25 percent of all state-owned industry, have been privatized. When Thatcher took office, nationalized industries employed 1.5 million people and dominated the transport, energy, communications, steel and ship-building sectors of the economy. By the end of 1986, more than 500,000 jobs—in excess of one-third of the total nationalized work force—had been transferred to the private sector.

The British have even gone so far as to privatize, in part, their social security system. Employers can contract their workers out of the second tier of the social security system by providing their employees with private pensions which assure retirement benefits as good as or better than those promised by government. More than half of all British workers have been contracted out.

The British privatization experiment has provided the world with a showcase for other nations to follow. And that, it appears, is exactly what other nations are doing.

Canada

The Canadian government has decided to sell two failing state-owned manufacturers, CanadAir and de Haviland, as well as mining businesses, including Eldorado Nuclear, a uranium producer. Canadian Arsenal, an arms manufacturing company, and Tele-globe Canada, which handles overseas telephone calls, also will be sold. In a statement announcing the privatization of these concerns, Robert R. De Cotret, chairman of the Ministerial Task Force on Privatization, said, "A key element of the government's commitment to good management is our policy for the privatization of commercial Crown corporations which no longer fulfill a specific public policy purpose."

France

Many sectors of the large corporations that the French socialists foolishly and disastrously nationalized after World War II are being sold. (Total losses of French nationalized industry for 1984 have been estimated at 37 billion francs.) For example, nationalized Renault has been selling a wide range of assets, including the company's prestigious Champs-Élysées headquarters, and Renix, an electronic component plant which was sold to the American company, Bendix. Nationalized Matra has sold its printed circuit subsidiary, Comelin, and its experimental robot modules plant, Robotronics—both to American buyers. Matra also has sold its machine tools subsidiary, MMA, and plans on selling its car division and its loss-making watch division.

Germany

At a cabinet meeting on March 26, 1985, the German government examined thirteen possible privatization schemes. They decided to concentrate on three general areas—industry, transport and banking. A portion of Berliner Bank already has been sold. Two smaller banks, some highway facilities on the Autobahn, trucking concerns and tourist offices are being readied for sale. In 1984 the German government reduced its ownership in the Veba energy group from 43.7 percent to 30 percent by selling 4.4 million shares.

Israel

Elta Electronics, a state-owned company which makes sophisticated military systems, will soon offer its common stock to the public. The government hopes to raise around $13 million from the initial issue, some 60 percent of which is expected to be purchased by the country's work force.

Italy

The socialist-led government in Italy also has begun to privatize. The Italian state holding firm, IRI, has raised $1.59 billion by selling some of its shares in various enterprises, including the AerItalia aerospace company and the Selenia electronics firm. Forty percent of Sirit, a subsidiary of the STET telecommunications company, was sold for 200 billion lira, and the state-owned Banco Nazionale del Lavoro, the largest bank in Italy, is offering 25 percent of its stock to private investors and an even larger share to its employees.

Japan

The Japanese, never slow to copy a good idea, have also begun to privatize their relatively small public sector. Legislation was passed in 1984 to transfer the telecommunications system, Nippon Telegraph and Telephone (NTT), as well as the state tobacco and salt monopoly, to the private sector. The profitable NTT became a wholly private company on April 1, 1985. Although privatization of the company was fought tenaciously by a combined bureaucratic and trade union lobby, the government pressed ahead because it felt that continuation of the company as a state monopoly would endanger long-term technological modernization.

The government will privatize the loss-making Japan National Railways (JNR) by splitting it into six private regional firms and two national private firms, one to own the bullet train network and the other, JNR freight interests. JNR's substantial land assets will be sold to pay off some of its debts. The government hopes to divest itself of other loss-making concerns as part of a wider strategy to reduce government spending and the budget deficit.

Privatization has gained a good reputation in Japan—good enough for the Minister for Aviation to propose that it be applied to Japan Air Lines (JAL) in order to restore public confidence shaken by the 1985 747 jet disaster. The Council for Transport Policy, a government advisory panel, proposed in December 1985 that the Japan Air Lines monopoly on international routes be ended, and that Japan's two other airlines be allowed to compete on all international routes. This policy is seen as complementary to the sale of JAL.

Portugal

The Social Democratic Prime Minister of Portugal, Anibal Cavaco Silva, has committed his government to a privatization program, blaming state domination of the economy for keeping the Portuguese standard of living behind that of most other European countries. In a speech announcing his intentions to the nation's Parliament, he stated: "Nothing justifies our remaining on the bottom rung in Europe. We are determined to put an end to the resignation and impotence imposed by our giant state machine."

South Africa

Even strife-torn South Africa turns to privatization as a means of invigorating its shaky economy. State intervention and regulation of the economy has been heavy. The public sector is a bastion of white privilege, with 46 percent of the 2.6-million white labor force being employed there. Recently, however, the South African government set up a special committee headed by three cabinet ministers to draw up proposals for the privatization of public sector enterprises. President P. W. Botha revealed that the government had been carefully studying the British privatization experience.

Three forms of privatization are under consideration in South Africa: the transfer of state enterprises into public companies, with shares issued through the stock exchange; the purchase by private companies of state assets on a tender of private allocation basis; and a management buyout option under which the management and employees of smaller state-owned companies would be encouraged to take over ownership.

Already Sasol, a coal gasification corporation, has been successfully privatized, and future privatization targets are expected to include South African Transport Services (which runs the state airline, the rail network, harbors and other transport services), Escom, the electricity supply corporation, and Iscor, the state steel corporation.

Spain

Although led by socialists, Spain has started a privatization program, with Prime Minister Felipe Gonzalez calling the bloated Spanish public sector a "white elephant graveyard." The national car manufacturer, Seat, has been sold to Volkswagen. Plans have been announced to sell a state-owned ball bearing factory and certain divisions of high-technology firms to the private sector.

It is expected that Spain's state airline, Iberia, also will soon be privatized. The state holding company, INI, has sold its textile firm, Textil Tarazona, as well as its stake in the Spanish subsidiary of SKF to the Swedish parent company. The Spanish truck- and bus-making firm, ENASA, has been sold to General Motors.

Sweden

The socialist government of Sweden has begun negotiations aimed at selling its 75 percent stake in Pripps, the country's leading brewery. Pripps controls 50 percent of both the beer and soft drinks market in Sweden. Although it had $329 million in sales last year, its market share has been declining since it was nationalized in 1975. (The government originally bought the company with the announced hope of changing Swedish drinking habits. It failed.)

Turkey

The Turkish government has sold the Bosphorus Bridge and the Keban hydroelectric dam. It also is planning to privatize 30 more state enterprises, including the state airline, THY. It is expected that an initial percentage of THY equity will be sold to the employees in the near future, with more of the equity being sold to the general public, followed by a final sale of shares to Turkish and foreign companies.

Privatization in Less Developed Countries

It may come as a surprise to many to learn that, aside from Britain, privatization has its strongest foothold in Less Developed Countries (LDCs). Widely viewed in the developed world as being hostile to capitalism and entrepreneurs, many of these countries are rapidly turning to private entrepreneurs and the profit motive as the key to economic growth. Privatization, in fact, may be easier in these countries because people in LDCs tend to be less reliant on government in the first place.

In the developed world almost all children are educated in public schools, while this is not generally the case in the less developed world. Similarly, whereas it is common in the developed world for travelers in large cities to rely on public mass transportation systems, it is the private sector that provides most mass transportation in large cities in much of the less developed world. In Buenos Aires, for example, private "microbuses" operate profitably and provide service that is widely

praised by visitors. In Cairo, privately owned taxis and
jitney services are relieving pressure on the city's over-
loaded network of bus and tram services. In Calcutta,
private buses operating without subsidies account for
about two-thirds of all trips. In Hong Kong, the service
provided by illegal (not government-franchised) mini-
buses became so popular that the government legal-
ized the vehicles in response to public demand. In
Manila, private "Jeepneys" are a major form of transportation, accounting for about half of all trips.

We tend to forget that most publicly owned utilities
in the developed world were once private firms that
supplied services people needed and were willing to
pay for. In many LDCs, there are a host of private
utilities that have not been nationalized. Caracas, the
capital of Venezuela, has been served by a private
unregulated electric company since the turn of the
century. Throughout the Philippines and Latin America, households are served by private (often competing) telephone companies. In Guatemala City, water is
completely provided by a for-profit water company.

Reliance on the private sector in the less developed
world is not merely a passive phenomenon, with the
private sector providing services which governments
either will not provide or cannot afford to provide.
Reliance on the private sector is rapidly becoming an
active, conscious policy of these governments. State-
owned telephone and telegraph companies are being
sold to the private sector in Bangladesh, Mexico, Thai-

land, South Korea, Malaysia and Sri Lanka, and airlines are being sold in a similar fashion in Thailand, Singapore, Bangladesh, Malaysia and South Korea. In a continuation of the privatization trend, state-owned banks are being sold to the private sector in Chile, South Korea, Bangladesh, the Philippines, Singapore and Taiwan, railways and bus services are being privatized in Thailand and Sri Lanka, while highways are being returned to private control in India and Malaysia.

The list goes on: Shipping and ship building are being privatized in Singapore, Bangladesh and Sri Lanka. Oil and petrochemical companies are being sold to the private sector in India, South Korea and the Philippines. State-owned hotels are being sold in Jamaica, Mexico, Singapore and the Philippines. Social security is being privatized in Chile. Sugar refining is being privatized in Jamaica and Uganda. Other general industries are being privatized in Argentina, Brazil, Chile, Sri Lanka, Pakistan, Singapore, the Philippines, Mexico, Peru, India and Bangladesh.

A Real Alternative

Like the developed countries, the LDCs are finding that state-owned enterprises are a net drain on their economies, and that by transferring them to the private sector a government can save money and at the same time create viable, profitable enterprises that contribute to economic growth.

Privatization doesn't eliminate services, it makes them better. With its amply demonstrated benefits, it can bring improved and cheaper services to the American public as well as to people around the world.

Stuart M. Butler

The Politics of Privatization

Privatization is rapidly becoming an everyday term throughout the world as country after country seeks to transfer government functions into the private sector, either to cut costs or—more often in the Less Developed Countries (LDCs)—to jump-start a flagging economy. The privatization campaign is most advanced in Europe, where France and Britain lead the way. In Britain, held back economically in large part because of widespread public ownership of industrial firms initiated after World War II, privatization began in earnest after the victory of Margaret Thatcher's Conservatives in 1979. To date over $20 billion worth of government assets and 600,000 public-sector workers have been transferred to the private sector—in an economy just one-tenth the size of that of the United States. World stock sale records have been shattered again and again as Britain sold major utilities and industrial firms to private investors. Companies such as Jaguar Motors, British Telecom (the nation's telephone system), the British Gas Corporation, and British Airways have been transferred to the private sector in multibillion-dollar stock offerings.

Many Asian countries have been following Europe's lead. Japan, for instance, has begun to sell its giant telephone system, Nippon Telegraph and Telephone, and is reorganizing Japanese National Railways with the goal of privatizing the system. And most LDCs are either undertaking the privatization of numerous government holdings or studying the strategy very carefully.

Local and State Experimentation

In the United States most privatization has taken place at the state and local level, in the form of contracting out the provision of government services to private suppliers. This form of privatization is now commonplace in American cities. For example, a survey by the Texas-based National Center for Policy Analysis found that approximately 35 percent of local governments use private firms to collect residential garbage, and 80 percent contract out vehicle towing. Other municipal functions routinely undertaken by the private sector include street repair work, traffic signal maintenance, data processing, ambulance services, health and welfare services, park landscaping and legal services. Moreover, a 1982 survey by the International City Management Association found a 50 percent rise in the number of American cities privatizing one or more services during the previous ten years. The number of firms used to collect garbage more than doubled during the period, private street repair operations rose over 600 percent, and the use of private firms to manage parks soared by a remarkable 2,700 percent.

Even fire departments and prison services are contracted out in some instances. In Scottsdale, Arizona, the Rural/Metro Company has provided fire service since 1949 for about half of the amount it costs in nearby comparable cities. Experts come from all over the U.S. and abroad to study the innovations Rural/Metro has brought to fire fighting. Some states are also experimenting with ways to save money through private prison services. They have been pushed in this direction by prison overcrowding and voter resistance to large expenditures for new public prisons. Corrections Corporation of America, headquartered in Nashville, Tennessee, operates low-security facilities for the U.S. Immigration and Naturalization Service, as well as a number of local jails, at a cost of about 20 percent less per inmate than the public sector can manage. Faced with massive overcrowding in the prison system, some states, including Tennessee, are even taking the first steps to explore the possibility of turning over parts of their medium- and high-security systems to private managers.

The idea of private enterprise operating prisons causes understandable concern for many Americans. Some find it hard to conceive of prisons run for a profit, and they are even more surprised and confused to learn that the Corrections Corporation of America is actually an offshoot of Hospital Corporation of America, a firm which constructs and operates medical facilities. Yet the marriage of hospitals and prisons is not so strange. The firms' administrators reasoned that there are striking similarities between operating low-security prisons and hospitals. From an architectural standpoint, both require structures in which staff can easily maintain surveillance over patients or inmates. Both involve a high turnover of short-term, unplanned "customers," imposing considerable accounting and organizational problems. And both require managers to arrange various ancillary services, such as catering and laundry. Thus the Corrections Corporation's background in hospital management has allowed it to bring very relevant cost-cutting skills to prison management.

More troubling to most Americans is the idea of a private firm making decisions about a prisoner's incarceration. Yet the function of private prison companies is strictly one of management. Decisions regarding the length of stay of inmates or the condition of imprisonment, such as solitary confinement, are left to officials of the penal system. And normally they provide no special services, such as counseling, unless these are prescribed and monitored by the prison system. Private prison firms simply house inmates, but do so in a more efficient manner than the public sector can.

Privatization at the local level has led to significant cost savings for cities. Study after study confirms that significant savings are possible when private contractors are employed. A recent study of the Los Angeles, California, area, for instance, revealed that street cleaning by city employees typically costs 43 percent more than the private alternative, and road resurfacing 96 percent more. Of eight services analyzed in the study, only in the case of payroll preparation were public and private sector costs comparable.

The secret behind the tremendous potential cost savings which privatization offers is twofold. First, there is the simple issue of competition. When city managers invite private firms to bid for contracts, they open up all sorts of possibilities for increased efficiency, better services and lower costs. Even if public-sector providers are not exploiting their monopoly power, there is good reason for expanding the options available. Secondly, cost savings are prompted by the fact that private contractors are not hamstrung by the political agendas which most public-sector providers have to include in their planning: factors such as employment goals, jobs for supporters, attention paid to key politicians, and so on. A manager at Amtrak, for instance, may recognize that given the small number of passengers using a particular station it would make economic sense to close it down. But he also knows that such a step would bring down the wrath of the local congressman and would, no doubt, mean that the station would be reopened. So it makes sense for him to swim with the tide.

It is no wonder that privatization has been proceeding at such rapid pace at the city level in recent years. City managers are more aware than ever before of the potential of private service delivery. Private firms specializing in such work have begun to approach more and more cities in an effort to attract business. This, in turn, has induced city managers to undertake studies to verify the savings that firms have been promising.

But a more important influence in recent years has been the budget pressure experienced by many cities. The deep recession of the early 1980s, combined with reductions in federal support instituted by the Reagan administration, have led to severe financial problems in most cities, many of which had explored the possibility of privatization earlier, but had ruled it out as impractical—usually because of the hostility of public-sector workers. Now, voter pressure to maintain services, along with a strong resistance to tax increases, has forced city managers to turn to more radical ways of cutting costs such as privatization. The privatization movement has gained momentum not because of some new widely shared ideological commitment, but because it has been the least painful option available to hard-pressed local officials.

Privatization Nationwide

At the federal level, however, progress towards privatization has been slow and halting, especially when compared to the British experience. To some extent, of course, this is because far less of the commercial economy is controlled by the U.S. government. Margaret Thatcher has a bigger task to face in disposing of publicly owned services, so her accomplishments understandably appear on a grander scale. On the other hand, the federal government does own considerable assets. Nearly one million acres of land are federally owned, as is a portfolio of loans to students, farmers and other groups, with a book value in excess of $250 billion. In addition, the federal government is the proprietor, either directly or through quasi-independent corporations, of the Postal Service, the Amtrak passenger railroad system, over a million public housing units, a system of electric power marketing facilities, thousands of buildings, and many other tangible assets.

The Reagan administration has on various occasions attempted to sell some of these assets, most notably small portions of federal land, together with Conrail, the power marketing administrations (which generate and market power derived from federal dams), and some portion of the loan portfolio. Yet without exception, these proposals have provoked bitter congressional opposition and most have turned into fiascos. Of the major initiatives, the only significant assets being transferred to the private sector are several billion dollars worth of federal loans, a small portion of the loan portfolio, and Conrail, which was sold to the public in the spring of 1987.

The reasons for this remarkably slow progress involve both institutional difficulties and strategic mistakes. In the first place, America does not have a parliamentary form of government. When Mrs. Thatcher presents a privatization proposal to Parliament, she can be virtually certain that her party's majority in the House of Commons and the tight party discipline which exists in the system mean that the proposal will easily become legislation—barring a revolt by party members or legal complications. Thus she can not only be sure that a sale will take place, but that a complex and sophisticated sale strategy will remain intact during parliamentary deliberations.

Not so in Congress. Placing a controversial privatization proposal before Congress is like throwing a message bottle into the ocean and hoping that it will reach some foreign land. Party discipline in Congress is very loose, and an administration's legislative program has to contend with shifting and unpredictable political alliances and factions. In addition, the business of Congress is heavily influenced by powerful committee chairmen who can block initiatives almost indefinitely—or demand the right to micromanage any proposal as the price of permitting a vote on the issue. Thus even a president as seemingly powerful as Ronald Reagan may be unable to prevail over a Congress that is unenthusiastic about an initiative, let alone hostile to it. If Margaret Thatcher had to deal with a similar situation in Parliament, there might be precious little privatization now taking place in Britain.

Thanks to the political dynamics of this unique form of government, eliminating a federal program turns out to be much more difficult than creating or expanding a program. As economists who belong to the "public choice" school teach us, the reason for this is because the benefits of a program are concentrated for a relatively small group, while the costs are spread thinly and widely over 100 million taxpayers, so the political balance always favors those who benefit from the program. The program beneficiaries have a strong financial self-interest to lobby hard for the program, exerting political pressure on lawmakers who are not tightly bound by party discipline. On the other hand, each taxpayer has very little financial stake in the outcome, and so although he may criticize federal spending, he is usually not inclined to expend time or money pressing for the elimination of any particular program. As Nobel laureate and leading advocate of public choice theory James Buchanan explains, that is why Americans say they are in favor of less federal spending but members of Congress rarely vote down programs. Any attempt to privatize, and thus withdraw the subsidies and other benefits that go with public ownership of an asset, is bound to run into stiff opposition. And since Congress is particularly sensitive to lobbying pressure from well-organized interest groups, trying to reduce the scale of government is extremely difficult.

The second cause of Reagan's failure to privatize more federal functions is his administration's seeming inability to learn from Mrs. Thatcher's experience. The conservatives turned what would have been a controversial initiative into a populist crusade by linking privatization with wide ownership of former government assets—public ownership was transformed into ownership by the public. In fact, most major privatization sales have involved an intense public relations blitz aimed at ordinary Britons. For instance, the sales of British Telecom and British Gas, each of which broke the world record for a stock sale, included heavy media advertising, with full-page newspaper advertisements carried day after day, and sophisticated television slots designed to build up investor excitement.

So far, the Reagan administration has not incorporated such aggressive tactics into its general privatization strategy. When the White House takes a privatization proposal to Congress, lawmakers hear quickly and loudly from its opponents. But they do not hear from anyone with a strong vested interest in a privatized program. Not surprisingly, the administration generally finds it very difficult to make headway.

The final reason why the Reagan administration has failed to move forward successfully with privatization is that so far it has not developed an effective procedure for managing the strategy within the executive branch itself, nor have officials learned from the British experience how to devise privatization initiatives in a way which reverses the dynamics currently frustrating privatization. Decision-making on the issue is not coordinated—it is spread throughout the administration. And in many cases, such as the attempt in 1986 to sell the power marketing administrations, departmental officials actually work against the White House. It is no surprise, therefore, that the opponents of privatization find it so easy to generate public criticism by misrepresenting the policy, or that they manage to outmaneuver administration efforts in Congress.

If the Reagan administration is to regain the initiative on privatization and score some successes in its struggle with Congress, it must learn the right lessons from British successes. In particular, administration strategists must formulate proposals which concentrate financial benefits on those who choose privatization over public ownership. As the British have shown, it is quite possible to detach or "buy out" powerful elements of coalitions committed to public ownership, and thereby weaken the political support for retaining functions in the public sector. Targeting benefits to other key groups can also help to build up new coalitions dedicated to the private option, which in turn become powerful lobbying constituencies for privatization. The Reagan administration would likely have taken far less than six years to convince Congress to privatize Conrail, for instance, if it had included in its proposal a plan to offer discounted stock to railroad employees and customers.

In addition, the administration must take steps to ensure that the right preconditions exist for privatization. This means centralizing and reorganizing strategic decision-making on the issue within the executive branch of the government. At the moment, White House planning primarily takes place within the Office of Management and Budget, which oversees all federal spending. But officials in each department are rarely brought into the White House to help develop a political strategy before the privatization candidate is announced. Invariably this leads to confusion within the administration when criticism is mounted against the plan.

The right preconditions also require that no concessions be made on the issue of raising taxes and that a continued determination to cut spending must be in evidence. The experience at the local level has been that budget deficit pressures have been the most effective stimulus for privatization initiatives. When a local official has to make sure that garbage is picked up to get reelected and he cannot raise taxes to pay for that service, cost reduction through privatization looks very attractive, no matter what his political philosophy happens to be. The same is true at the national level. With a president determined not to raise taxes, Congress on a self-imposed timetable to reduce the deficit (thanks to the Gramm-Rudman-Hollings legislation), and with each lawmaker anxious to keep services flowing to his constituents, privatization looks increasingly like the best if not the only political option available. Indeed, in the case of Conrail, it was only the attraction of nearly $2 billion in sales revenue that prompted congressional action on privatizing the railroad, not some deep commitment to the philosophy of smaller government.

Similarly, it is hard to persuade government employees or the beneficiaries of government services to consider privatization unless there is a Sword of Damocles—in the form of the threat of budget cuts—hanging over their heads. Otherwise they have every incentive to ignore privatization proposals and support the status quo. Only placing them in budget jeopardy effectively encourages them to consider the alternative of privatization.

Fine-Tuning the Strategy

Changing the incentive system to foster privatization thus involves creating proposals which concentrate benefits on key groups of beneficiaries, service providers and other constituents necessary to forge political coalitions committed to privatization. These coalitions would be, in effect, "mirror images" of the coalitions of beneficiaries and other interest groups that currently lobby for public ownership and service provision.

There are several ways in which privatization benefits can be conceived in order to energize these coalitions. Each of these has different uses and implications.

Spreading Ownership

Using a form of sale that allows the ownership of an asset to be distributed means that a political constituency can be created to support the sale. The Thatcher strategy of giving preference to small investors, for instance, has helped to build a bulwark against possible renationalization by a future Labor government. By contrast, the Reagan administration initially sought to sell Conrail to a single buyer, the Norfolk–Southern Railroad, and so a relatively small constituency had a direct stake in the outcome. Political problems quickly followed. It was only when the administration accepted the idea of a public stock offering that congressional opposition began to crumble.

Tactical Asset Transfers

In addition to the general approach of using asset transfers to generate a base of support, a portion of an asset may be given or sold on favorable terms to a key part of the coalition supporting public ownership, in order to break down its opposition to privatization—and perhaps even turn it into a strong advocate of the policy. The awarding of stock to employees of nationalized firms in Britain has served to neutralize labor opposition and win over management. And the transfer of public housing assets to tenants decisively changed the political dynamics, forcing even the opposition Labor Party to accept the policy.

Tactical ownership transfers could be highly effective in breaking up public-spending coalitions in the United States. Many conservatives were surprised, for instance, by the degree of support they have received from inner-city residents for the idea of selling public housing to tenants. In the future, the administration might look at transferring some of the assets of, say, the Postal Service to its workers to give them a strong ownership stake in privatization and to buy out their current generous pensions. Similarly, free-market environmentalists Richard Stroup and John Baden have aroused considerable interest in their plan to reduce opposition to the privatization of public lands by giving wilderness lands to environmental organizations.

Their aim is to turn the debate over privatizing federal lands by detaching the most powerful element in the opposition lobby.

Worker Ownership

Transferring a government asset or service into the hands of former government workers has also proved to be an effective way not only of altering the political dynamics but also of improving the economic efficiency of the firm. Britain's National Freight trucking company, for example, was turned over to its workers in 1982. With their new slogan, "We're in the Driver's Seat," the worker-owners promptly put an end to the featherbedding and costly work rules that had kept the firm in the red for years. Within five years productivity had risen to the point where each worker's stock was worth forty times its original value. In America, a worker buyout might do similar wonders for the Postal Service.

The idea of worker ownership could also prove decisive in the battle for privatization in Less Developed Countries (LDCs). In many such countries there is political antipathy to the notion of private ownership and a fear that a lack of domestic capital resources might make privatization synonymous with a transfer of control to foreign buyers. Worker ownership may be the antidote. It suggests socialism, and yet it is simply shared capitalist ownership. And by transferring ownership rather than selling an asset on the open market, the fear of foreign domination is removed.

Contracting Out

At the state and local level, the main form of privatization has taken the form of governments contracting with private firms to provide service. This remains the simplest and most attractive form of privatization in the case of services, and it is likely to spread at all levels of government in the United States. But it does have its dangers. When the service to be performed is very specialized—such as sophisticated weapons research or certain welfare services—the private providers will usually try to reduce the degree of competition by pressing for licensing and other restrictions on entry. This allows the private providers to charge higher prices and so reduces the potential gains from privatization. At the extreme, the group of private providers may actually form a powerful lobby to win approval of increased total spending on the service. So a policy of contracting out services is likely to be most successful when the service is of a routine commercial nature, where the private providers are not price-setters. In the case of more specialized services, steps must be taken to ensure the maximum degree of competition.

Tax Benefits

Tax incentives can be used to provide a concentrated benefit where there are no assets to transfer. The tax benefit rewards those who choose the private option or who provide the private service. In this way a strategy of "parallel" privatization may be developed, in which the existing government program is not confronted head-on, but instead an alternative private program is established and allowed to grow. Eventually, the political support for the alternative is used to offset support for the public sector program. The establishment in the United States of the Individual Retirement Account program in 1982, under which taxpayers can deduct from taxable income contributions to private pension programs, has enabled workers to begin building up a private supplement to Social Security. Although the deduction was restricted somewhat in the 1986 tax law, the fierce resistance against complete elimination mounted by the IRA lobby demonstrated the power of the tax-induced constituency. There can be little doubt that pressure to restore and expand the deduction will not be long in coming. Ultimately the parallel private pension system could grow to the point where its constituency could become a powerful counterweight to the coalition which backs the Social Security system.

Creating and Recognizing
Privatization Lobbies

Current beneficiaries of government programs usually devote a portion of their benefits to maintaining associations and lobbying organizations to further their interests. But even if a presidential administration proposes a model designed to stimulate the growth of a privatization coalition, the forces of privatization initially will be at a disadvantage compared with this existing coalition. They will not be organized—they may not even be aware of each other. Until the benefit is actually transferred, any financial "investment" they make in lobbying will be purely speculative, so they are less inclined to finance a campaign.

If the campaign for privatization at the federal level is to acquire new strength, it is necessary to recognize and reinforce potential networks for each privatization initiative. This can be done in various ways. Devoting research funds to discovering and organizing potential beneficiaries, for instance, can plant the seeds of a powerful coalition, and awarding new organizations the status of an official body can be critically important in changing the terms of the public debate. The Left has been very successful in creating a cadre of official "spokesmen" and "citizen groups" to promote the cause of expanded government. Privatization strategists should do likewise to further the goal of limited government.

The privatization approach thus differs markedly from more traditional ways to reverse the growth of government. Most advocates of smaller government engage in a war of attrition, which they invariably lose because they try to marshal many—but unenthusiastic—voters against a determined, self-interested coalition. The beauty of privatization is that it changes the options made available to individuals. It alters the political choices they make by offering them incentives to choose the private sector, *diverting* their political demands rather than trying to block them. And that is why it holds such promise as an antidote to runaway government spending.

Dick Armey

The Road Away From Serfdom

Although I currently serve in Congress, I regard myself as a free-market economist—a price theorist and a microeconomist, to be precise. Yet I was not introduced to the work of great free-market theorists like Ludwig von Mises or Friedrich von Hayek as an undergraduate or even as a doctoral student. Indeed, it is safe to say that *Human Action* and *The Road to Serfdom* are rarely read in American universities while books like John Kenneth Galbraith's *The Affluent Society* is widely read and discussed as if the Great Society programs it rationalized were not in total disarray today.

Why do some economic theories remain popular even when the policies and results they have wrought are under serious question? I have been acutely aware of the answer to this inquiry ever since I discovered as an academic professor that macroeconomics is typically more popular than microeconomics: easy ideas are always more quickly accepted than hard ideas. Galbraith's ideas, which were always more like scenarios than science, made their way into our government, our schools, and our entire way of thinking because they were so easy to grasp and to explain to others. As much as any other reason, this is why I ran for political office: to help in some small way to undo the damage Galbraith has done.

Recognizing Constraints

Galbraith set forth the notion that the American economy required a "social balance" which would mean the transference of the control of our resources, from the private to the public sector. He, as much as Lyndon Johnson, was the architect of the Great Society. He ignored the reality that things only happen when someone makes the decision to do something, that the world revolves around choices. Every choice is between what Samuelson called the "minima" and the "maxima," but even extreme positions must be chosen within a limiting set of constraints.

The trouble with Galbraith's theory and, ultimately, the greatest evil of *The Affluent Society* is his refusal, replicated by President Johnson in his ill-famed guns-and-butter speech of 1965, to acknowledge this basic truth. There are no limits, no constraints, they claimed instead, so we don't have to be careful about husbanding and allocating our resources among competing ends. Today you can witness many government policymakers in action who don't recognize even the most ordinary constraints in the way you or I would. We are all intimately involved, for example, with the principle of budget constraint, sometimes called "fiscal responsibility." If we spend more money than we earn, the check at the grocery store bounces and then our car may be repossessed or our house . . . we face direct and unpleasant consequences for our profligacy. Does anyone really suggest that the government fears the same?

Each and every day of our lives tells us that there are constraints on time. This is, perhaps, the most fundamental and universal fact known to man: life is temporary, limited. Yet our government's lifespan is hardly measured in the same terms.

Another vital and undeniable constraint is scarcity. What makes gold precious is that there is so little of it to be had, and the same goes for any other resource, whether it is water, energy, concert pianists, or life itself. We are limited in all that we do and all that we seek. Yet Galbraith and many of our government representatives would have us believe otherwise. They play upon our resentment of those richer or more successful than ourselves, a resentment articulated many years ago by Thorstein Veblen in his highly influential book *The Theory of the Leisure Class* which painted the upper strata of our society as indolent, self-indulgent and hoarding.

The modern redistributionists don't carry their dog-eared copies of Veblen or Galbraith in their back pocket, but they don't need to; they've already been given the intellectual framework from which they can operate. Their first task is to convince us that we're not running our economy or our lives well enough on our own. We need their help, they argue. "Look at the terrible shape America's in. The problems are too big for individuals to solve. Let us help." And they offer us, simply, more government—more government along Keynesian lines with many instruments of what I refer to as "government by deception," not the least of which is deficit spending, in which the true costs are hidden from the people who, of course, pay the bills, or through another instrument, corporate taxation, which is sold to the voters as if it had nothing to do with their own incomes.

The Great Society changed the nature of government spending and taxation—in short, the whole landscape of our economy. But we have lost more than money in the process. We are no longer able to distinguish between the legitimate roles of the private and the public sector, and, more often than not, it is the wrong one which is characterized as irrational and inefficient.

How to Think About the Deficit

Right now we have a lightning rod in "deficit ma-
nia." So, since people rarely understand the real problem, we might as well educate them about the symp-
toms. The deficit, let me stress, falls into the symptom
category; but it may be the best "two-by-four" with
which to hit people over the head when it comes to
making them understand our larger dilemma. Even
Democrats who have never been, even by their own
admission, feverent budget-cutters, are making fiscal
responsibility a headline issue today.

But our true task does not lie in eliminating the
deficit. (Considering how Congress usually spends
money, the interest paid on the deficit may be its
all-time best investment.) We have to cut the size of
government. Bring it back to its proper size. Put it in its
place. This isn't an economy measure—it is absolutely
necessary if we are to continue to thrive as a constitutional democracy. But in a highly practical way, the
deficit can be the tool we use to convince others who
don't understand.

Restoring limitations on federal power is not easy.
When Congress or the administration tries to cut
spending, critics call them heartless and claim that the
critically needy will suffer. The wise allocation of resources will lose out every time when the choice is
presented as between government services and no ser-

vices at all (as if the private sector didn't exist). This is motivated by the Keynesian presumption that if government doesn't do it, it won't get done, and if the government doesn't spend money on worthwhile programs, the money won't be spent and the programs will collapse. *That* is how far we have come in two hundred years.

Privatization

Privatization has become the great safety valve, especially for conservative politicians, Republican, Democrat or otherwise. Transferring a very small number of services back to private hands one at a time is far less traumatic and far more feasible than trying to reduce the size of government in a frontal assault on whole agencies or departments. In Congress, a privatization task force of which I am a member has been gaining influence, and public concern about the deficit has been a key advantage. The task force outlines three basic methods of privatization. One is contracting out certain services. Private companies, for example, may bid on running commissaries on our defense bases or computer work or printing jobs that may be handled more inexpensively and efficiently by outside firms. The second alternative is asset sales. This along with the third method, selling loan portfolios, can be much harder to follow because of the high visibility each entails. When it comes to privatizing railroads, public utilities, federally owned buildings and the like, critics are ready to call it a "fire sale." With unbelievable audacity, some say, "You want to sell the *government's* property to the *people* of this country?" (And that is the stuff which sells in Washington.) Transferring the ownership of property or services to private control on the basis of rational market decisions and clearly defined objectives is often misrepresented as robbing the government or even "the taxpayers" (an entity some refer to as equally unconnected to actual individuals), but nothing could be further from the truth.

Armey's axiom number one: The market is rational. The government is dumb. That is not merely a cliché. I used to teach an entire graduate course in order to reinforce such a premise. Individuals face sobering constraints every day—money, time, resources—and they do not, on the whole, make heedless decisions.

We taxpayers (and I do mean we individuals) pay $650 to $700 million dollars a year to subsidize passengers riding Amtrak. Is this rational? Of course not, and when the case is this extreme, as with the deficit, people do understand and respond.

Armey's axiom number two: You don't have to be a conservative to want to get the government off your back. Two black leaders with whom I met recently, both women who have been lifelong Democrats and public housing tenants, agree. If we privatize public housing, will people be homeless? No, they say, give the poor vouchers and they will find their own cheaper residences. One of these women said, "I don't want the government rebuilding the plantations." She understands that she does not want the federal bureaucracy as the slum landlord of the '90s and she does not want to be its victim. The lesson is obvious. What this woman desires is the protection of her right to make her own decisions; hers is not an ideological passion.

In the last few years, the congressional task force on privatization created several bellweather proposals, of which loan portfolio sales were our flagship. We felt we could build a constituency behind them very quickly and with minimal political resistance. Of all of the proposals, "urban homesteading" is, perhaps, the most appealing. People who now live in what we call "the projects," government housing that's been mismanaged and which is falling down around their ears, have been reduced to wards of the state. We must give these people the opportunity first to organize and manage their own buildings and then to buy their own homes. Home ownership carries with it a strong sense of responsibility and there is no doubt that it helps families stay together. When fathers own their own homes where are they? Out carousing? No—they're home with their heads under the kitchen sink, or painting the walls, or fixing the shingles, or doing the yardwork. Teen pregnancy rates drop dramatically too, and often homeowners band together to drive out drug dealers in neighborhoods where urban homesteading initiatives have been implemented.

A recent article in *The Washington Post* comments on these privatization initiatives by noting that fathers who return to participate exhibit a surprising number of skills the welfare and housing "experts" never knew they had. Plumbers, carpenters and electricians abound. As tenants of public housing, these men were forbidden to make improvements by statutes requiring all repairs to be made by union workers at prevailing wages. Naturally, few tenants were willing to pay for repairs or take an interest in the condition of housing which did not belong to them.

As a freshman congressman, I experienced far less success with the idea of postal privatization. Persuaded that I could have an influence on my peers in Washington, I hired a private postal carrier to send a "Dear Colleague" letter to all the members of the House. The letter began, "This letter is being sent to you illegally. But I could deliver it to you for *five cents* a copy. . . ." The United Postal Workers Union was outraged, and I couldn't convince Congress to go along with postal privatization then; however, every year privatization of all sorts of "sacred cows" like the postal service, Amtrak, health care and so on, is becoming more attractive to an increasing number of Americans. The biggest roadblock is the Democratic Party, even though its individual members are often in favor of privatization. Why? Because in 1965 federal spending, previously only for capital goods, was expanded to include consumption goods with the intent to redistribute wealth along the lines drawn by Galbraith, Johnson, and the Great Society. This kind of spending has bought whole constituencies and has created, ultimately, the Dependent Society.

Less Government is More

We must not simply attempt to cut federal aid. Democrats and Republicans alike will fight for their constituents who crave and demand aid. What we must do is to offer these constituents something better than a "free lunch"; we have to convince them that privatization will bring direct benefits and mean more opportunities to share the American dream.

Politically, what ought to arise out of the privatization movement is not a realignment of power but a reversion to an older way of thinking, that less government is more: more economic prosperity to go around, more creative energies unleashed, and a more responsible, self-reliant and independent people. This democratic republic was founded in order to guarantee equality of opportunity and the freedom and dignity which comes from being one's own person. For a government to try to do more is to jeopardize the very rights it aims to protect. I want to reiterate that privatization is not just a passing economic fancy or a way to trim the deficit; it calls for a restoration of ideals badly needed if we are to prosper as individuals and as a nation.

J. Peter Grace

The Problem of Big Government

There are 2.7 million federal employees in the United States, occupying 2.61 billion square feet of office space, the equivalent of all of the office space in the ten largest cities multiplied by four. These are astonishing statistics for a country which claims to be guided by the principle that government ought to play an extremely limited role in men's lives. It is even more surprising that we tolerate such an enormously bloated bureaucracy when everywhere in America it is recognized that the public sector simply does not work as well as the private sector and, furthermore, that it is small private organizations which work better than big ones.

With all the serious problems we must face today, the problem of big government is among the most critical. Yet solutions are not lacking; most of them are readily understandable and of a practical rather than an ideological nature. For instance, at least 600,000 civil service jobs are completely unnecessary, and the President's Private Sector Survey on Cost Control recommended in 1984 that they be privatized immediately. The survey recommended a few other reforms, too: 2,478 of them to be precise. But only a small number of these have been implemented. Why? One of the reasons lies in the fact that the federal government is controlled by Congress. Rarely do people realize how many day-to-day actions of the government are affected by the 535 elected members of Congress who micromanage each agency and thus exert a powerful influence beyond their legislative function.

Let me illustrate. Several years ago, John Shad, head of the Securities and Exchange Commission, was able to streamline the time-consuming and labor-intensive registration process for the corporations it regulates. Consequently, he was also able to cut his staff, or RIF (reduction-in-force) as it is commonly called, 230 employees. Two days later, he was summoned before the congressional subcommittee responsible for overseeing the SEC.

"Why are you RIFing 230 people?" he was asked. He gave them a reasonable explanation.

"Come back to the chairman's office, and we'll talk about this for a few minutes." He was presented with a list of items he had included in his agency's operating budget for the next year. "Do you want cooperation on this budget?"

"Yeah, I have to have this budget."

"All right, then cancel the RIFs."

"Okay, I'm learning."

So it goes in Washington, D.C. Look at the exorbitant freight rates for the Defense Department's operations in Alaska and Hawaii: $68 million was spent over a recent three-year period. Why? Congress does not permit competitive bidding for shipping military freight to and from the mainland for these two states. The average middle-American family pays $2,218 in taxes. So it is fair to assume that 34,000 families are working all year long to pay that $68 million.

NASA puts out a highly successful magazine which is oversubscribed (General Electric alone requests 5,000 copies each month), but the Office of Management and Budget (OMB) insists upon limiting production. Some time ago, the editors declared their intent to solicit advertising in order to print the magazine privately. Going private would also mean a great savings—proofreaders from the Government Printing Office are paid $32,000 a year and can look forward to retiring on 82 percent of their final salary. Ordinary proofreaders, in comparison, make about $15,000 and have little or no pension benefits outside of Social Security. But another subcommittee reared its head and prevented NASA from going ahead. Coincidentally, most of the subcommittee members who decided against privatizing the magazine were senators whose constituents included a disproportionate share of civil service employees, many of whom worked for the Government Printing Office.

The head of the Veterans Administration is also under the thumb of Congress. Changing the jobs of three employees requires that a written request be submitted by February 1, and Congress has until October 1 to respond. Micromanagement is, perhaps, too mild a term to describe what Congress is doing to our government.

The Defense Department has certified that the United States needs 326 military bases: we have 4,000. These include Fort Collins, built to protect Salt Lake City from the Indians, and another installation in Virginia which still has a moat around it. A move to turn it into a museum was blocked by the congressional delegation from . . . need I tell you? Virginia. Typically, the congressmen who complain loudest about the defense budget are the same ones who cavil at such sensible ideas as reducing the number of active military bases. Absurdity leads to absurdity. You have undoubtedly heard of two-cent screws bought for $91.00, $7.50 hammers for $435.00, and toilet seat covers for $678.00—all due to the specifications which Congress has imposed. The Defense Department makes roughly 1.5 million purchase decisions each year. It hardly needs the kind of help Congress has to offer.

Perpetual Debt and Deception

Pertinent today is Thomas Jefferson's warning, "To preserve our independence, we must not let our rulers load us with perpetual debt." He added, "We must make our election between economy and liberty . . . or profusion and servitude." We are spending $220 billion more than we accumulate in revenues each year. We face a debt of $2.2 trillion. Now, you cannot really conceive of a trillion dollars and neither can I. We can figure out the calculations, of course—a million million, a thousand billion—but that is not really going to help us to understand. If someone started ticking off the seconds since the time of Christ's birth, today the count would be at a little over 65 billion, with less than seven percent of the task finished. It takes 31,700 years to count to a trillion, or 317 centuries, and we are only in the 20th. But in Washington, D.C., "trillions" is a commonly used term and some of our civil servants don't even bother with that; they casually refer to "trills."

I've been a businessman long enough to have experienced the horrors of unbridled government indirectly for years, but since 1982, when President Reagan approached me about heading up the Private Sector Survey on Cost Control, later known as the Grace Commission, I have been able to relate many incidents firsthand. At the outset, he asked me to discover the answers to a series of questions. One of the primary ones, prompted by his former governorship of California, was to find out how many federal employees worked in California. During his own tenure, he knew that they outnumbered state employees but was unable to discover anything more concrete. As president, he felt that it was important to pursue the issue and find out not only how many federal employees there were but where they were located and what they were doing. The day after our conversation, I went to the OMB and asked those three simple questions.

"We don't know" was the answer, and I could not get any specific data. So I changed my tactics.

"If I can't present the White House with a complete report by next week, I will hold a press conference and tell the American people that there are 2.7 million federal employees in the United States and that the OMB hasn't got the slightest idea of where they are or what they're doing."

The bureaucracy relented and I received a massive computerized listing of the number of federal employees in each state, but that was all. I went to Edwin Meese, then the Counselor to the President for Domestic Affairs, who earnestly tried to help, but more than three years later, I am still waiting for the answers to the other questions President Reagan asked.

I made other sallies at the OMB in the meantime, asking logical questions like, "How many social programs does the government sponsor?"

The answer was "110 to 130."

One of our staff visited a bookstore soon after that and came across a revealing volume called *How to Get Yours In Fat City.* In the appendix, 300 government social programs were featured. We took this interesting information back to our OMB sources, but they were unimpressed. We conducted our own research and dug up a total of 963 social programs. They are all formularized in Congress and many of them are called "entitlements." Keep that word "entitlement" in mind because, if you're not getting anything, you're a sucker—you're "entitled" to a lot of these programs. You can enroll in 17 of them simultaneously and draw 160 percent of the minimum wage.

Now, W. R. Grace & Co. owns, among other things, 740 restaurants. One waitress I visited with in New Orleans makes $130 a day just in tips. Not everyone who waits tables makes this much, but say they make $50 per day, three days a week. That amounts to $150 a week in tax-free income, and if they are making 160 percent of the minimum wage from government social programs to boot, they are enjoying a very tidy setup. For those of us who declare our incomes, the underground economy is an affront, not only because it means a loss of over $100 billion in tax revenues a year, but because these people are on the dole at the same time they are evading taxes.

Student loan programs are also a haven for fraud. Our commission decided to investigate and found that there are three separate student loan programs. "Why have three?" we said. "How much is their overhead? Is it possible for them to merge into one program?" Aside from the usual recalcitrance displayed by federal agencies, we came up against another obstacle, one which we had encountered in every one of our investigations: the federal government's 332 incompatible accounting systems and 319 payroll systems, all handled by 17,500 computers, 12,000 of which were obsolete. When I found that out, my reaction was "Let's get Frank Cary down here"—the chief executive officer of IBM at the time, a businessman known for his expertise and his integrity.

I called Frank up and he said, "Sure, I'll be there."

Congress cried, "Conflict of interest! He knows too much!" and Frank Cary, along with many other committed, expert volunteers like him were denied the chance to help our Commission. But eventually we were able to determine that approximately $2.5 billion in defaulted student loans had not been collected. Who owed the money? People like a Mets pitcher and a Honolulu land developer and, among others, 46,000 federal employees. Now maybe $2.5 billion does seem like a small percentage of the $850 billion in outstanding loans owed to the government at the time, but it is certainly not outrageous to suggest that these folks ought to make good on their legal obligations.

Earlier, I noted that the debt stands at $2.2 trillion, but I was lying to you, just as Congress always does. Another trillion dollars in the Social Security system and $1.1 trillion in military and civil service pensions account for past liabilities which have not been recognized or provided for. Social Security is a nightmare you probably already know a lot about, but did you know that the military retirement program is exactly six times as generous as comparable private programs? A man or woman entering at age 17 can retire in 20 years with 50 percent of his or her salary indexed, of course, to inflation. During President Carter's term, we endured two years of 13.2 percent followed by two years of 11.6 percent inflation. Let us estimate that over an extended period inflation levels out to about 7 percent. In ten years, a pension settlement will double. At age 47, a military retiree will receive 100 percent of his final salary each month; at age 57, it becomes 200 percent; at age 67, doubling to reach 400 percent, and so on. This is not a pension plan; it is a bonanza.

Federal civil service employees may retire with very similar benefits, so it is no wonder that unfunded pension liabilities exceed $1 trillion. Added to all the other hidden debts Congress refuses to tell its citizens about, the real debt is between $4 and $5 trillion. When President Lyndon Johnson launched the Great Society he was already committed to a war in Vietnam. His administration spent $158 billion. Now, that sum is only the interest on the national debt. That is some "legacy" for our children. I saw a cartoon recently which featured a bunch of politicians having a meal in a restaurant. The headwaiter brought the bill and they replied, "Stick it on the kids' tab." And that's what we are doing. We are just sticking it on the kids' tab. What right do we have to live this way? How can we go on spending so much ($400 billion more than we took in last year including all the off-budget expenditures) when we know where our folly will lead?

The Real Job of Government

The Grace Commission effectively demonstrated that $424.4 billion could be saved over a three-year period by following its 2,478 specific recommendations. Moreover, the Commission showed its own commitment to cost-cutting by raising $76 million from private organizations to underwrite all of its own expenses. It did not cost the government a nickel, unless, of course, you agree with Ralph Nader. He claims that at least half of the study was paid for by the government because the donors were able to deduct their contributions, costing millions in lost tax revenue. Tax evasion does account for lost revenue as I indicated in the case of the underground economy, but Ralph Nader is unsafe at any speed when he suggests that your pre-tax income belongs to the government and that by giving any of it away to a commission, a church, or any other charity you are bilking the government out of its rightful due. That is socialism, plain and simple.

Unfortunately, socialism has far too great a hold on us already, and anybody who disagrees ought to look

at those 963 social programs the government has bur-
dened us with. When Kennedy was President, he was
our King Arthur and he reigned over Camelot, but
Camelot's social programs, $38.5 billion worth, were
only 5.8 percent of the Gross National Product (GNP).
Reagan, who has been called Scrooge, presides over a
$486 billion social agenda which swallows up 13.5 per-
cent of GNP.

Kennedy spent 9.4 percent of the GNP on defense
and Reagan, by contrast, spends less than 7 percent. In
the last 70 years, the communists have succeeded in
subjugating 1,727 billion people, or 36.1 percent of
the world's population. They have taken over 18.7
million square miles of territory—that is 32.5 percent
of the earth's land surface—in the process. Reagan's
commitment to defense notwithstanding, 7 percent of
the GNP seems wholly inadequate.

The Soviets have produced twice as many fighter
aircraft as we have together with our NATO allies.
They have also manufactured four times as many heli-
copters, five times as many artillery pieces, twelve
times as many ballistic missiles and fifty times as many
bombers. In the area of short-range missiles, Soviet
forces have a 14.6 to 1 advantage. In intermediate-
range missiles, the ratio is 1.2 to 1, and in strategic
missiles it is 1.5 to 1. Remember the awful destruction
caused by Hitler's 43 submarines in World War II?
Well, Russia has 300, 150 of which are nuclear and 8 of
which are circling off the coast of Florida right now.

In short, the threat to our freedom is not diminishing. The real job of government is not to give us 963 social programs but to protect our liberty. We ought to be living up to the principles of our forefathers. We ought to be vocal about waste and fraud in government. We ought to be asking each and every one of our representatives in Congress: "Why are we keeping 4,000 military bases open? How many federal employees work in my state and what are they doing? What are *you* voting for and voting against?"

Our Future Is At Stake

In 1984, when the Commission officially presented its findings to President Reagan, it was during a White House conference. One of the questions addressed to me from the group of nearly 200 reporters on hand was "Why isn't there anything in your report about taxing the rich?"

I explained that we were not asked to examine the tax structure, that it was not within the perimeters of our investigation. I asked my interlocutor a question in return.

"Who's rich?"

"Anybody who makes more than $75,000 a year," she replied.

I said, "You're right; $75,000 is rich."

But at the Democratic Convention that same year many of the candidates were calling for a 10 percent surcharge on the incomes of those who *they* claimed were rich—the people earning $60,000 a year. At the time, our Commission figured that this initiative would collect only $1.65 billion a year, or eight-tenths of one percent of the deficit. Why were the Democrats cheering in the aisles at this kind of talk? Because economic illiteracy, jealousy and envy are the fuel that politicians run on.

I told the reporter about what the Democrats had pledged and I said I would go them one better. "Let's put a 100 percent tax on all incomes over $75,000 a year."

She said, "That would be good."

And I replied, "Fine. Now we'll be able to run the government for 7.2 days."

Taxing the rich is not the solution; adopting waste-cutting measures like the ones the Grace Commission proposed is. When New York City went bankrupt, it had no choice but to attempt to put its fiscal house in order. But the trouble with the federal government is that it simply cannot go bankrupt; it will just print more money or borrow more. Now, if I'm having an argument with a congressman and we talk about spending $1.00 and I say "You can knock it out" and he says, "No, I'm leaving it in," I respond, "Where do you get that buck?"

He says, "Tell Jim Baker to borrow it over at the Treasury."

"Where does he get the interest?"

"Borrows it."

"Where does he get the interest on the interest?"

"Borrows it."

"Next year it's $1.05. Where does he get that?"

"Borrows it."

Well, take a little calculator out and figure out what happens when you borrow something, then you borrow the interest, and then you borrow the interest on the interest. In our report to President Reagan, we warned that one dollar borrowed now will have cost $71.00 by the year 2000. In a little more than 12 years, the debt will be $13 trillion and the interest on that will be $1.5 trillion. By the same token, if the Commission's recommendations were followed, we could save $9.9 trillion.

We need a knowledgeable, informed electorate that doesn't depend on the nightly news for what it knows about what goes on in this country. We need citizens willing to make Congress accountable for the travesty which passes for democratic government today. Until we have them, we will continue to be bamboozled by Congress which, in its turn, knuckles under to the bureaucratic establishment and the 500 special interest groups entrenched on Capitol Hill. We can start by making the government fiscally responsible, but whether we can muster the political will to do so is up to us alone.

The stakes are high; what kind of future can we build for ourselves unless we mend our ways? What kind of future for our children and their heirs will big government and institutionalized fiscal irresponsibility yield? What we are committing now is child abuse on an unimaginable scale. When our sons and daughters grow up and realize what we've done to them, will they ever forgive us?

Allan C. Carlson

Privatizing the Family

In his great work, *Socialism,* Ludwig von Mises describes how the state uses philosophy, bound to opportunity, in order to expand its domain into hitherto private spheres of life. A principal target, he shows, has been the family, and the marital bond at its core:

> Proposals to transform the relations between the sexes have long gone hand-in-hand with plans for the socialization of the means of production. Marriage is to disappear along with private property, giving place to an arrangement more in harmony with the fundamental facts of sex. When man is liberated from the yoke of economic labour, love is to be liberated from all the economic trammels which have profaned it. Socialism promises not only welfare—wealth for all—but universal happiness in love as well.

Seen from another angle, a primary goal for socialism has been destruction of the private home, of the autonomous family. The critical functions of the family—economic, educational, nurturing, reproductive, emotional, religious—must be stripped away, one by one, and socialized. As Marxist philosophers have long understood, this dismantling of family life would have economic consequences, too, for it is the family which takes the rough edges off dynamic capitalism, that creates oases of stability and love in the midst of capitalism's "creative destruction," that sets up boundaries to egocentricity and acquisitiveness, channeling those qualities into constructive rather than destructive ends. Without the institution of the autonomous family, socialist thinkers have long understood, capitalism would self-destruct.

This allows us, in my opinion, to turn to the "privatization" model as a useful way of thinking about social policy and family policy. While typically used to describe the process whereby modern welfare states divest themselves of the ownership of goods and resources, privatization and especially the phrase, "privatizing the family," allows us to focus on the close relationship between a free economy and the family, and to recognize the common danger posed to both by the aggressive State.

Roots of the American Family

We should begin by understanding the philosophical origins of the Western Judeo-Christian concept of the autonomous family. It was not the relatively recent creation of the bourgeois capitalist, as the socialists have charged. Rather, the philosophical roots of the autonomous family lie deep in the history of our civilization.

Our concept of the "private family," as so much else, was born with the philosopher Aristotle. While rejecting Plato's utopian vision that called for a shared community of women and the abolition of the family, Aristotle did respond to Plato's views in his *Laws*. Human beings are innately social, Aristotle argued, and at the root of human society "must be a union of those who cannot exist without each other; namely, of male and female, that the race may continue." The marital bond grew into the household, "the first" social institution, which merged with other homes into villages, and the villages into the State. While in a metaphysical sense, Aristotle saw the State as prior to the family, "since the whole is of necessity prior to the part," it remained true, he stipulated, that the State was composed of households, enjoying a certain natural autonomy.

A long succession of Christian theologians adopted this understanding. In the fifth century, St. Augustine, the famed Bishop of Hippo, labeled the family composed of man, woman, and children as the only "natural bond of human society." The State, in contrast, was to be feared. "What are kingdoms but great robberies?" He wrote "For what are robberies themselves, but little kingdoms? The band itself is made up of men; it is ruled by the authority of a prince; it is knit together by the pact of confederacy; the booty is divided by the law agreed on."

Thomas Aquinas, the great Medieval theologian, regarded the state in a somewhat better light. While newborns depended on families for their birth and early nurture, he qualified, the State also "provide[d] public services beyond the means of one household, and for moral advantage." Aquinas was clear, though, that the State was a servant of, not the lord over, the natural bonds of the family.

Sixteenth-century reformer Martin Luther emphasized that marriage was the first and primary social bond, the natural community ordained by God for procreation and for the renewal of society, but he also saw the State as an imperfect, albeit necessary, device, also instituted by God to maintain order, to prevent or punish vice, and to protect homelife.

In more recent times, too, this ecumenical tradition has found affirmation. As Pope Leo XIII declared in his 1891 encyclical *Rerum Novarum:* "Behold, therefore, the family, a very small society indeed, but a true one, and older than any polity! . . . For that reason it must have certain rights and duties of its own entirely independent of the State." Leo denounced efforts by governments to displace the family, to weaken marriages, or to undermine parental authority. The natural freedom of the family, he said, must be maintained.

The American experience gave special emphasis to the private nature of the home. From the English common law, Americans drew the notion of the home as a place of shelter and privacy. In a case before the Court of the King's Bench in 1605, Sir Edward Coke explained the meaning of the tradition: "That the house of every one is to him as his Castle and Fortress, as well for his Defense against Injury and Violence, as for his Repose." Restrictions were placed even on state law officials, as to their ability to invade private homes. Rhode Island's 1647 Legal Code, for example, forbade "forcible Entry and Detainer." The officer of the law could break open a house under stringent conditions, "but not in the execution of a process upon the body or goods of any man . . . for a man's house is to himself, his family and goods, as a castle."

Furthermore, geography enhanced this legal commitment to family privacy and autonomy in America. The hunger for land was so great that the early colonists built their villages on large lots. Andover, Massachusetts, in the 1640s, for example, consisted of 22 lots ranging from 4 to 12 acres in size, and resembling nothing so much as a modern suburban housing development. Only Boston took on the characteristics of a European town, but even there—witnesses said—the gardens lent "a sense of spaciousness." Indeed, the ordinary colonial family enjoyed a particular intimacy, encouraged by its physical separation from others. As a female resident of Cambridge, Massachusetts, reflected in 1768: "Can there be a happier Seene, than nature display'd in Rural life, free from all the noise and dust of a city, surrounded with your Little ones, Tasting the sweets of domestic peace?"

The privacy of the family and the protected nature of the home blossomed over the course of the 19th century. The conventions of the middle class home took form in the writings of women like Catherine Beecher and L. H. Sigourney. In a world dominated by commerce and industry, they said, the home was the oasis or refuge, a place of love, intimacy and joy, a private sphere designed for the fulfillment of life through marriage, children and Christian service.

Yet the enemies of the autonomous family were already gathering, and began mounting an attack that one commentator has labeled "sweeping and unremitting." Using the privatization model, we can see that this assault on the autonomous family, usually in the name of the state, has occurred for reasons identical to those long used to justify state restrictions on the economy. As Mises has shown, though, this ought not surprise us: the free-standing family is the social foundation of the free economy; the latter cannot survive without the former. State intervention has assumed four main forms. What follows is a discussion of each.

The Statist Mentality

Beginning with the 17th-century philosopher Thomas Hobbes, an important strain of secular liberal thought emphasized the negative tension between the individual and the family, and the need to use state authority to free persons from their family. As Hobbes put the matter in 1642, man is not, by nature, a social animal. Rather, he said, that "all society is either for gain or for glory; not so much for love of our fellowes, as for love of our selves." Maternal love is no more than the "dominion over the infant" by stronger mothers; while the honor shown parents by children is simply "the estimation of another's power."

John Locke, it is true, worked to put a more human face on a society of competing individuals, and he was able to carve out a role for parents in the birth and early care of children. Yet he saw the individual will as still supreme, and marriage as little more than another contract, appropriately dissolved or weakened as the children grew up.

In the 19th century, other theorists in the secular liberal tradition professed similar hostile or ambivalent attitudes toward the private family. John Stuart Mill, for example, found the family structure of early Victorian England to be repressive: for women it was "the equivalent of slavery"; for children, "the seedbed of despotism." In our time, bearers of the liberal philosophic tradition, scholars like John Rawls, have emphasized the tension between the liberal principle of "fair opportunity" and the family. "Is the family to be abolished then?" he asked in 1971. "Taken by itself and given a certain primacy, the idea of equal opportunity inclines us in this direction."

Liberal suspicion of the family has left the institution vulnerable to the more extreme statists, the common descendants of Jean-Jacques Rousseau. On the one hand, Rousseau helped shape middle class sensibilities about family life through his famous novel *Emile,* the book which, among other results, reintroduced breast feeding to the French aristocracy and bourgeoisie. Yet his fully developed political views left no room for the family. As he wrote in his essay *On the Government of Poland:* "the newly born infant, upon first opening his eyes, must gaze upon the fatherland, and until his dying day should behold nothing else." Love for and obedience to parents, in particular, should be superseded by the State.

The intellectual "children of Rousseau," to borrow a phrase, have been numerous. They include the German socialist August Bebel, author of the popular volume *Women Under Socialism* (1883), who portrayed the female sex as the group most victimized by capitalism, brutalized in the workplace and abused at home. The destruction of the private household is the prerequisite for social progress, he said. Friedrich Engels, Karl Marx's collaborator, agreed that human freedom would only be won through elimination of the private home, with marriage abolished, child care provided by the State, and other household tasks such as food preparation transferred into the industrial economy.

Some American Progressive reformers shared a similar vision. Historian Arthur Calhoun, for example, wrote in his 1918 work *A Social History of the American Family:* "The new view is that the higher and more obligatory relation is to society rather than to the family; the family goes back to the age of savagery while the state belongs to the age of civilization. The modern individual is a world citizen, served by the world, and home interests can no longer be supreme." That is almost pure statist gospel, and such sentiments helped to justify the growing intrusions of government into the home.

In the Name of "Freedom"

The second and related reason for State intervention has been that the abuse of freedom by some becomes a justification for restricting the freedom of all. With the growth of government regulation, isolated instances of improper behavior are usually the stimuli which lead to laws or regulation restricting everyone's liberties; so, too, with families. In the mid-19th century governments in France and the United States first grew consciously aware of how children in a family could serve as a valuable lever of social control. The charge against parents, of course, was always neglect, abuse or inadequacy. Sometimes these acts were indeed real. Oftentimes, however, they were not, for the purpose behind the reform campaign was broader. In their ability to remove or merely threaten to remove children from their families, the State and its growing legion of allied philanthropic societies found a powerful weapon to impose conformity and control. At first, the targets of these campaigns were found almost exclusively among the laboring classes, and the poor.

In the United States the government's regulation of families took shape around the *parens patriae*—or "parenthood of the State"—argument, one of the more insidious doctrines to seep into our legal system. By the 1830s, social reformers were building reform schools in most states, to which judges were remanding children for incarceration without jury trial, without attention to the rules of evidence, without access to legal counsel, and for an indeterminate sentence. In 1839 a father secured a writ of *habeas corpus*, seeking the release of his daughter from the Philadelphia House of Refuge. The managers of the institutions— early so-called "child savers"—fought the writ, arguing that the Bill of Rights did not apply to children or families. The Pennsylvania Supreme Court agreed, citing in addition the doctrine of *parens patriae*. This ancient concept was drawn from British chancery laws justifying only the Crown's assumption of the parental role in order to protect the estates of orphaned minors. Yet the Pennsylvania court, in looking for a legal device to get around due process, extended the doctrine for the first time to the termination of parental rights. "May not the natural parents, when unequal to the task of education or unworthy of it, be supplanted by the *parens patriae,* or common guardianship of the community?"

State welfare professionals and their friends at court now had a tool of enormous power in their hands, one which led to ever broader claims of authority. As the Illinois Supreme Court, in a sweeping judgment, ruled in 1882:

> It is the unquestioned and imperative duty of every enlightened government, in its character of *parens patriae,* to protect and provide for the comfort and well-being of such of its citizens as, by reason of infancy, defective understanding, or other misfortune or infirmity, are unable to take care of themselves. The performance of this duty is justly regarded as one of the most important of governmental functions, and all constitutional limitations must be . . . understood . . . so as not to interfere with its proper and legitimate exercise.

Understand that last phrase: even the rights guaranteed by the Constitution must not be allowed to interfere with the government's efforts to save the family from itself, or the individual from himself.

Indeed, the claims of the child savers have known no bounds. During the 1920s the most prominent theorist of the movement was Miriam Van Waters, who argued in her book *Parents on Probation* that "hardly a family in America is not engaging in the same practices, falling into the same attitudes, committing the same blunders which . . . bring the [juvenile] court families to catastrophe." Parents could no longer "shield themselves behind *natural* rights," she said. It was "only a question of time before the parents' psychological handling of his child" would also be subjected to the scrutiny of the State. She looked forward to that great day when *every* parent would be in the embrace of the therapeutic arms of social workers to "willingly cooperate in a plan for his own welfare," and then face "the super-parent, which is mankind," with a "face stained with tears," saying: "Sure, I'll make good."

The actual system of governmental control changed over time. In the 1830s and 1840s, the primary institution was the reform school. Industrial training schools rose to dominance later in the century. Between 1898 and the early 1920s most states created juvenile court systems. During the same era, the Eugenics movement stormed to power, and 15 states implemented laws to sterilize, with force if necessary, so-called "feeble-minded" children. Over 50,000 youthful Americans, guilty of no crime other than being a little slow, were sterilized by the child savers and reformers before that fad mercifully ended. Since the early 1960s a massive and still growing campaign against child abuse has given the State's disruption of families new force and urgency. New reporting laws in all 50 states have stripped away still more legal protections from families: husband-wife and physician-patient privileges are denied; immunity from civil or criminal liability is granted to accusers; parents are essentially assumed to be guilty until they can prove their innocence. Federal and state governments are also setting up teams of experts to go into schools and ferret out "potential" abusing families. These teams are authorized to examine a family's income, history, "attitudes," self-image, parenting skills, and impulse control. If parents do not measure up, their children can be seized. In 1986 alone, an estimated 1.5 million American families were subjected to the indignities and subtle terrors of a State investigation into their character.

The "Public Crisis"

The third reason for State intervention into families has been the periodic "public crisis." Much as the economic crisis of the Great Depression led to new government controls over productive activity, so have a series of "social crises"—real or contrived—drawn the State ever further into the family.

Juvenile crime, perhaps, has been the champion public crisis. During the 1890s, the 1920s and the

1950s, concern welled up over the rate of youth crime, reaching in each case panic proportions, and new methods of intervention were contrived to solve the problem. While working mothers and divorce rates were regularly absolved by the experts of any responsibility (these, after all, were so-called favorable trends), the family was commonly blamed for the problem. As sociologist Harry Shulman put it, the "weakening of parental decision in a hundred small issues taken together has led to a social revolution in manners and morals." Most observers shook their heads and commonly agreed that attempts to reconstruct the "old values" of family and religion would never work. Social change, they said, demanded creative "social construction" through the mechanisms of the State.

We can see the same process at work in our own time. We all know, for example, that the United States is currently in the midst of a great "youth suicide crisis." Our television news commentators and our popular magazines tell us so. Yet the "crisis" label cannot survive a real look at the facts. It is true that the youth suicide rate rose 150 percent between 1955 and 1977. But the more important fact is the rate has been *declining* since then. Moreover, while each self-inflicted death by a young person is an undoubted tragedy, the aggregate numbers involved are fairly small. In 1975, for example, in a nation of 225,000,000 people, the total number of suicides among 5-9 year olds was zero (there weren't any); among 10-14 year olds, 170; and among 15-19 year olds, 1,594. Viewed internationally, the problem also shrinks. Among young males, the U.S. suicide rate is only half of that found in Switzerland and Austria, for example. Among girls, the U.S. rate falls below that of Denmark, France and Japan.

Nonetheless, our opinion leaders and Congress are moving quickly toward setting up a federally funded national youth suicide prevention program. Its advocates ignore the mass of research indicating that the probable cause of the rise in suicides between 1957 and 1977 can be explained by three factors: a decline in church attendance by youth; rising divorce; and the movement of mothers into the work force. Rather, for the advocates of State action, "cause" is a mystery. The intervenors are only sure that family and religious renewal are ineffective solutions. Instead, they call on the State to intervene in family life with "home visitations," to examine "intrafamilial communications along characterological lines." They also pledge to establish "substitute families" in the public schools, led by the able advice of professional intervenors.

Teenage pregnancy is another of our great contemporary crises, demanding state solutions. As matter of fact, there are no more teenage pregnancies today than there were 30 years ago. What *has changed* is that, whereas in 1957 over half of pregnant teenagers would find their way to an altar and marriage, fewer than 15 percent do so today; and whereas the child of an illegitimate birth would in 1957 have most likely been put up for adoption, our current welfare system and mores allow and even pressure the unmarried teenager to keep her baby.

Those who believe that new governmental programs of sex education and contraceptive training will reduce teenage pregnancy have to face certain uncomfortable facts. Youth sex clinics, for example, claim to be able to reduce teenage birth rates. Recent studies suggest, though, that this occurs only through a dramatic rise in the number of abortions. At the heart of federal sex control programs, though, lies a central demand: children must be freed from their parents' control on matters involving sexuality; they must be taught their values by the State; they must be given their choices by the State. So once again, we find a "crisis" serving as midwife to the further corrosion of family bonds, and to the joint elevation of the radical individual and the all-encompassing State.

An Economic Rationale

State intervention into the family has also been instigated by a perceived "market failure." The inability of the marketplace to solve certain problems has been a common rationale for state regulatory intervention, particularly in the environmental arena. So, too, with the family economy.

Early 20th-century critics of industrial capitalism, on the political right as well as the left, agreed on a common complaint: the incentives found in a totally free labor market would tend to undermine traditional family bonds. In contrast to the preindustrial era, in which the farm economy and guild restrictions sheltered the family's interests, the industrial order undermined the position of skilled male labor. Manufacturers found that women and children were equally capable of running the machines, and were usually cheaper to hire. As members of a single family were drawn into competition with each other, critics said, family life would unravel. Moreover, they noted, competitive wages took no account of family size. A bachelor, a man with an employed wife, and a man with a wife and five children at home each received the same wage, yet the latter family subsisted at a much lower standard of living.

Attempts to restore a "living wage" for families in a market economy took two forms. In the United States reformers argued for three mutually reinforcing goals: laws ending child labor; legal restrictions on the paid work of married women; and payment of a "family wage" to male heads of households, an amount sufficient to support a typical family of five.

However, this limited accommodation to the economic pressures on a family was flawed. During the 1920s, for example, American labor leaders based their wage demands on "the family of five" standard.

However, fewer than half of male workers at any given time actually had dependent children at home, and less than one-fifth had three or more. Economist Paul Douglas calculated in 1925 that paying all adult male workers a wage sufficient for a family of five meant supporting 48 million fictitious dependents. Moreover, this semipublic method of delivering a family wage rested on institutionalized discrimination: the assumption that women's labor would be treated as secondary or supplemental.

These arguments of efficiency and equality drew most governments further into the family economy. As English analyst Eleanor Rathbone concluded, the only consistent solution to the family wage problem was a state system of family allowances "that will, once and for all, cut away the question of the maintenance of children ... from the question of wages." This compelling logic led all Western governments, except the United States, to create allowance programs as part of their respective social security systems. Put another way, the "market problem" of the family was solved by making all families wards of the State.

Reprivatizing the Family

From studies of government regulation conducted over the last several decades, we know that state ownership or control of resources and activity produces numerous inefficiencies, distortions, and unintended consequences. State attempts at governance of the family have had similar disheartening, if predictable, results.

Studies of the family intervenors and of the nation's juvenile courts have yielded similarly grim tales. In his history of attempts to control juvenile delinquency, for example, Robert Mennel found a system of unredeemed "drudgery and debasement," where "institutions and juvenile courts smothered decent instincts and encouraged further crime and deviance." Other historians including Anthony Platt and Michael Katz have outlined the same story: the programs of the child savers have diminished constitutional liberties, disrupted families, and often aggravated the very problems such programs were supposed to solve.

The same tragic tale continues in our day, the only change being that where the child savers once confined their attentions to persons of color, the poor and the immigrant, the middle class is now also at risk. In 1985 alone, up to 1,000,000 *innocent* American families were accused of child abuse and subjected to State scrutiny, many seeing their children seized by therapists and held for extended periods of time. Such new pressure is fueling the rapid growth of grass-roots organizations such as VOCAL—Victims of Child Abuse Laws—which now has chapters in most states, a dozen in California alone.

There is growing evidence, too, that the very act of

State intervention into families that *are* abusive merely worsens an already bad situation. When State intervention disrupts family integrity, the child's needs are denied and his security shaken. As three eminent psychiatrists have concluded: "The law does not have the capacity to supervise the fragile, complex interpersonal bonds between parent and child. As *parens patriae* the State is too crude an instrument to become an adequate substitute for flesh and blood parents."

To take another example of the political law of unintended consequences, the payment of state allowances to families has been, at best, a mixed blessing for parents; at worst, it has simply granted the State another means of undermining family liberties. In France, for example, a new mother's mandatory visit to the family allowance bureau allows welfare officials to open a file on the family, recording information on its structure, income and history. In addition the State's concession of an allowance gives social service agents the legal right to intervene in families without warrant or other authorization. In Sweden the child allowance program has been used as a crowbar for ideological purposes. The decision to funnel all checks through the child's mother, for instance, was purposefully taken to reduce the father's influence within each family.

Facing these forces that gnaw away at family autonomy and threaten human liberty, how might we move toward reprivatizing the family?

To begin with, we might place some hope that the court system may someday sharply restrain the work of the State intervenors. While the dominant legal precedent has been to support the intervenors and reduce the protections afforded families, there has been a strong and encouraging line of dissent. In 1965 the U.S. Supreme Court, in its controversial *Gault* decision, dealt a crippling blow to the *parens patriae* doctrine in the field of juvenile delinquency. (Although, much like the March of Dimes in search of a new disease after the conquest of polio, social welfare officials appear to have simply turned their interventionist tendencies toward a "new" problem: child abuse.) More recently, former Chief Justice Warren Burger declared for the court majority that "the statist notion that governmental power should supersede parental authority in *all* cases because *some* parents abuse and neglect children is repugnant."

Similar good sense can also be found at the state level. In a stunning 1982 decision, for example, the Utah Supreme Court struck down a provision of that state's Children's Rights Act, which allowed for the complete termination of parental rights if determined to be "in the child's best interest." Writing for the majority, Justice Dallin Oaks declared that the parental right to rear one's child "transcends all property and economic rights. It is rooted not in state or federal statutory or constitutional law, to which it is logically and chronologically prior, but in nature and human instinct." (Aristotle, Augustine, Luther and Leo XIII would have cheered here.) Justice Oaks was appalled, in particular, at the presumption of state officials to know with certainty what was "best" for children. There was no surer way to destroy authentic pluralism, he said, than by terminating the rights of parents who violated the "trendy" definitions and "officially approved values imposed by reformers empowered to determine what is in the 'best interest' of someone else's child."

Second, we need to see and work toward direct and real cuts in the size, funding and power of the specific therapeutic agencies that make up our matriarchal, semisocialist state. Budget reductions in the areas of "family services" and "child protection" will predictably bring howls of protest and charges that legislators are abandoning children to the inhuman monsters who are or might be their parents. Such cries are best countered by investigations, legislature- or media-led, into the thousands of specific cases of state abuse of children and families. The neglect and abuse laws in the states need also be rewritten. Existing incentives that reward welfare authorities for an increase in unsubstantiated allegations need to be eliminated; the ancient legal protection of parents, including the common law presumption in favor of the reasonableness of their actions, also needs to be restored.

Third, to the fullest degree possible, we need to "voucherize" existing state welfare services. Such devices, which give benefit recipients the equivalent of cash to spend among a range of service providers, would be most applicable to areas such as care of the severely handicapped, day care, and counseling. The political importance of vouchers derives from their ability to reverse partially the existing power relationship between the state welfare official and the client family.

Fourth, the "family wage" problem posed by a market system can have a nonstatist resolution. In place of state allowances funded by extra taxes and processed through a state's treasury and bureaucracy, the same rough result can be achieved through a series of tax credits and deductions keyed to number and age of children. Measures could include: first, a major increase in the tax exemption for dependent children, to $4,000 per child; second, expanded eligibility for the Earned Income Tax Credit, which currently allows the working poor, with at least one child in the family, to recover a portion of their payroll or FICA tax; or third, creation of a universal child credit, set at $600 per child and available up to the total value of the payroll tax; and fourth, transformation of the existing child care tax credit into a universal credit available to all families, including those which care for their own preschool children. Under this scheme, families would retain more of their earned income when they have children, without interfering with a competitive labor market and without subjecting themselves to possible new manipulation by government authorities.

Early in this century, Theodore Roosevelt described his great nightmare for the American future: "Doctrinaire Socialism," he warned, "would replace the family and homelife by a glorified state free-lunch counter and state foundling asylums ... with the abandonment of all morality as between man and woman." We are probably closer to that nightmare world than we would care to admit. Behind that charge lie statist ideologies that have progressively undermined the place of the autonomous family in our civilization, and an aggressive bureaucracy that has made war on the family, using the same justifications that have drawn the State into the economy.

The free economy, in the end, depends on the free family for its social harmony and biological continuity. Mises' words, quoted earlier, indeed seem prophetic. He warned us decades ago that socialism is not merely an attack on our economy but upon every aspect of our lives. The alternative to reprivatizing the family can be starkly drawn: the final socialization of families and childrearing, and the continued destabilization of a free and responsible people.

George Marotta

The World Stock Market: Financing Privatization

I am very pleased to report that the results of my research indicate that "privatization," the sale of government-run enterprises to the investing public, is being very efficiently funded throughout the world. Coming from the Hoover Institution at Stanford University, located in the heart of California's "silicon valley" where entrepreneurship is running rampant, it is very difficult not to be optimistic about current trends. There, the constant merging of risk capital and talent leads one to believe that this phenomenon is being, or can be, replicated everywhere.

Fortunately, as of this writing, booming stock markets around the world are aiding in the smooth absorption of the shares of these new private businesses in the developed countries. Further good news is that the benefits of capitalism and privatization are obvious worldwide—even in communist China. Less happily, there are no well-developed stock markets in many poorer countries to permit the volume of sales of government-controlled enterprises required to vitalize their economies, and it is not only in countries like China that anticapitalistic policies and actions are flourishing; they have strengthened their hold on the U.S. economy as well.

But for my part, I still prefer to emphasize the good news. Everywhere there is recognition that government bureaucracies are the most inefficient form of organization for delivering goods and services: government monopolies foster unresponsiveness, pay increases beyond market rates, lost tax revenues, reduced competition, and lowered incentives for needed reforms and productivity gains. Most people need no persuading that the "market" is a better delivery system than government. Privatization, where it has been implemented, is visibly providing better and lower cost service as well as a reduction in government debt and increases in tax revenues. To these multiple benefits is added the gains from increased public ownership of private enterprises—in other words, a healthy spread of "people's capitalism."

First, I would like to examine the stock markets throughout the world: in the United States, the other mature industrialized nations, the newly industrialized countries, and finally in the developing countries.

The United States

The stock market in the United States serves as the intermediary for the participants of capitalism. Some look at the daily gyrations of the stock market and see only a jumble of figures, but it is possible to dissect the data and derive many clear messages about the economy, industries, and individual companies. It's exciting to read about the final accounting of millions of individual decisions. It is our daily report card on American business activity.

The market went straight up in the first three months of 1987, advancing about 400 points or 21 percent as measured by the most popular and closely watched index, the Dow Jones Industrial Average. By the spring of 1987, it doubled what it was just a year and a half before. What is the market trying to tell us? We can detect several messages. Most importantly, stocks love falling interest rates which have been declining steadily since the double-digit levels of the early 1980s.

The market, if I may refer to it as a single entity, also likes lower inflation. In 1985-86, inflation was at its lowest level in decades—1.1 percent. In "real" terms the stock market at the 2,300 level in the Dow Jones Industrial Average is still below the 1,000 level in relation to 1973 dollars. The market also likes stable and lower wage rates. Cooperation, rather than confrontation, between management and labor has increased productivity in the United States. Companies that are doing best are those with enlightened and harmonious labor relations.

The stock market is euphoric about the new tax law. Because of the lower marginal tax rates, we can now spend less time sheltering income from taxes and can get on with the business of making investments which have an economic rationale. The market likes the decline of the dollar against other major world currencies, although we would prefer that it not drop too far. Soon, we hope, our export levels will increase as American goods, when measured in foreign currencies, will decline in price. We can't do worse in 1987 than we did in 1986—a $175 billion trade deficit.

The market also likes the restructuring of American business, which our relatively free economy has fostered and encouraged. Resources are being transferred to better use as outside managers threaten entrenched managements with takeovers, mergers, and similar developments. All this activity simply adds to the evidence that the price of many company shares is still undervalued. So far, government has kept out of this healthy process.

The American market is very attractive to foreign investors. Some Japanese brokers are recommending to their clients that one-half of their equity portfolios be invested in U.S. stocks. Moreover, all of this increased demand is taking place while the supply of stocks is being reduced because of the growing number of mergers, leveraged buy-outs, and corporate stock-repurchase programs.

The market, at an all-time-high level, is good news not only for stock owners but also for workers (more jobs), management (security and higher pay), the needy (more tax revenues for social programs) and society's general well-being. It is also good news for the advocates of privatization. The healthiness of the stock market has, for example, made easy the absorption of shares in our denationalized railroad freight business—Conrail Corporation. This was the largest initial stock offering ever made on the New York Stock Exchange and augurs well for other similar initiatives.

The World Stock Market

The total value of all common stock in the United States is about $2 trillion. Outside the United States, there is $4 trillion in additional equities in the world's 14 largest industrial countries. Foreign stock markets represent a large portion of the world's common stock investment opportunities.

How does one invest in overseas securities? There are several ways: purchase of the company stock through a foreign broker; purchase of the company stock through a U.S. broker by buying American Depository Receipts traded on U.S. securities exchanges; buying closed-end investment funds; and purchase of open-end investment fund shares.

There are 56 foreign companies listed on the New York Stock Exchange, 49 foreign companies on the American Stock Exchange, and 260 foreign companies on the over-the-counter market. Foreign company trading represents 8 percent of all of the over-the-counter NASDAQ trading.*

There are many closed-end mutual funds on the stock exchanges which invest in securities of one country. Italy, France, Japan, Korea and Mexico have funds which are listed on the New York Stock Exchange; and funds from Australia, Scandinavia and Taiwan are on the American exchange.

The largest category of foreign funds is the open-end variety, those which issue new shares upon receipt of additional monies. Some of these funds represent pools of several hundred millions of dollars and are growing at a very rapid rate. Each mutual fund group now has a fund which invests in overseas companies. For example, the Fidelity group has the Overseas Fund, Price has the International Fund, Vanguard has a World Fund, and Scudder has an International Fund.

To illustrate the rapid proliferation of investments in overseas mutual funds, I counted 24 such funds in a study two years ago, 48 last year, and 82 now (24 of which invest in precious metals).

---

*National Association of Security Dealers Automated Quotation System.

The main reason for investing in overseas companies is that such investments will probably produce a higher total yield in the future due to more rapid growth. It must be recognized, however, that about half of the gains over the past two years were due to the dollar decline against other currencies. The best performances in overseas investing by open-end mutual funds in 1986 were Fidelity Overseas with a gain of 69 percent; Price International, 62 percent; Vanguard World, 57 percent; and Scudder International, 51 percent.

Since 1970, all major foreign stock markets have outperformed the U.S. stock market. Because of strong demand for equity shares, governments in the United Kingdom, France, Italy and elsewhere have been able to carry out and accelerate their "privatization" programs. Although foreign stock markets have performed better than ours since 1970, the job creation record of the United States during this decade has been the envy of the world—particularly the European countries.

Meanwhile in the United States the media typically concentrates all of its attention on the negative indicators—the unemployment rate, for example, instead of the employment levels. We have successfully created over 10 million jobs this decade for high school students, college students, "reentry" women workers, and so on, but the media persists in looking at the "hole" which is unemployment rather than the "doughnut," which is increased employment.

Developed Countries

Governments throughout the world have had to ration shares of common stock in the sale of government-owned industries because of eager buying, frequently by first-time investors. In France, the denationalization program is one of the most popular actions of the conservative Chirac government. The common stock of privatized industries has been reasonably priced and has been gobbled up by the French. Some issues have been oversubscribed by as much as 65 times, leading one French investment analyst to comment that "we are really seeing the creation of popular capitalism here for the first time. Everybody is now interested in stock." Denationalized industries include electric power, advertising and communications, banking and television. Thus far, over $10 billion has been added to the French treasury, and an additional $40 billion will be raised during the five-year sales program.

The British sale of denationalized industries has been so successful that they are hoping to become a model for others to emulate in revitalizing an economy. The sale of such giants as British Telecom and British Gas can only help solidify the position of Margaret Thatcher because the price of shares of the denationalized companies have risen almost 60 percent higher on average than the index of U.K. stocks in general.

The Italian government is selling off large chunks of government industries on the Milan stock exchange and has sold $3 billion worth of IRI—the state conglomerate Instituto per la Recostruzione Industriale.

Third World Countries

If one does not invest abroad, he is limiting his investment potential, and is actually increasing risk because of a lack of diversification. The securities game is going global. In addition to the mature markets in New York, London, Paris, Milan, Tokyo and Zurich, stock exchanges are flourishing everywhere. Examples include Hong Kong where exports are strong and the economy is very healthy, Thailand where the underlying economy is strong, and Korea and Taiwan, which are the fastest growing but are off-limits to investors except through closed-end mutual funds.

There has been a tremendous surge in stock markets throughout the world in recent years. Some countries, observing a close correlation between a well-developed stock exchange and growth, are planning to foster the development of this intermediary institution.

The Third Wave

As a financial planner, I frequently recommend that a person interested in investments read Alvin Toffler's book, *The Third Wave,* which I believe best explains the major trends that are occurring. The first wave refers to an agricultural base, subsistence living, and a lack of specialization whereby each individual tries to do everything to take care of his needs. The first wave is characterized by poverty, the condition under which a majority of the world's population still lives.

In the second wave, the industrial revolution, machines amplify the individual's muscle power. The specialization of labor and mass production dramatically increased the United States' standard of living. Of the droves of farmers who left their fields for factory jobs, most gladly exchanged the harsh and unpredictable farm life for the certainty of relatively "easy" 12-hour work days. The second wave was facilitated by the magic of the corporate structure and capitalism. The corporate structure permitted the marriage of capital, labor and professional managers within a framework of limited liability. Patent protection spurred innovation, and the financial equity markets facilitated the efficient transfer of ownership shares.

We are now deep down the unknown path of the third wave which is the service industry society. This is the "brainy" wave—characterized by technology and our expanding ability to communicate instantly anywhere in the world. Much of the recent wealth created in the world is due to the fantastic levels of trade which are taking place—currently at the annual rate of almost $3 trillion! The magic of trade is that both parties benefit. It is not a zero-sum game. All countries have some "comparative advantage" in that each can export something that it can produce efficiently in exchange for something that someone else can produce efficiently.

We in the United States are extremely lucky that our comparative advantage is based on three important third wave components—computation, communication, and high technology. The fact that we have the comparative advantage in these areas is demonstrated by constantly declining costs of production. Stated another way, our productivity in these areas is increasing at a rapid rate.

Two-thirds of the countries in the world—about 100 former colonies—have gained their independence since World War II. Although many adopted democratic political systems, most soon drifted toward some form of authoritarianism. After a brief flirtation with the form but not the substance of democracy, they quickly came under one-man or one-junta or one-party rule. Also, because of inexperience and uncertainties, most retained central control over their economies.

The widespread nationalization of businesses in Third World countries provides one of the greatest opportunities for privatization. Unfortunately, these countries have the least-developed mechanisms to finance the sale of government-run industries to the private sector.

From a practical standpoint, it is in our self-interest to help the poorer countries to denationalize their industries. We know that the way to create wealth is to create incentives and to rely on the market mechanism rather than the constraints of undue government interference. If we help poor countries to develop, we can do more than open new markets, increase trade, and create new jobs; we can help spread hope and build a climate in which freedom can flourish.

Poor countries want capital to expand job opportunities. However, most do not like the "idea" of capitalism, and especially fear the power of multinational corporations and other "economic imperialists." Therefore, the infusion of private capital investments from many different sources into existing private companies might be more welcomed than investments from concentrated sources.

Developing the economies of Third World countries is extremely important to the United States. About 30 percent of U.S. corporate profits are derived from international trade and investments. The Third World countries have accounted for most of the growth in our exports in recent years. One of every three farm acres produces for export, with one of five going to the developing countries. One of every eight manufacturing jobs depends on exports, one of every six jobs in nonmanufactured goods, and one of every thirty jobs in services.

The United States will always play an important role in foreign assistance to poorer countries and in achieving foreign policy goals. The basic goals for foreign aid have changed dramatically over the decades. Starting with the Marshall Plan in Europe, we later shifted our emphasis to the provision of technical assistance, and then toward the construction of large infrastructure projects within the targeted countries. In the 1970s, Congress required that U.S. foreign assistance be redirected toward meeting basic human needs. The shift from a top-down to a bottom-up mode was met with many frustrations and failures. Now it is time to redirect efforts again.

Rather than a government-to-government approach or a government-to-people approach, we need to emphasize direct support of local businesses in poorer countries in order to provide growth and jobs. Emphasis on private enterprise is the most rapid and efficient economic development approach. Also, a market-oriented economy will lead to maximum individual freedom and will support the development of democratic forms of government. The President's Task Force on International Private Enterprise in a December 1984 report urged that "the U.S. Government to the maximum extent feasible should channel its foreign assistance resources through the private sector and not through governments."

Third World Mutual Fund

The newest and one of the most exciting innovations regarding the Third World is the inauguration of mutual funds that will invest exclusively in the companies in that area. The first such fund is the Templeton Emerging Markets Fund, a closed-end mutual fund traded on the American Stock Exchange. The World Bank helped to launch this fund, as it did Korean and Taiwanese funds.

To illustrate the demand for these foreign closed-end funds, the Templeton Emerging Markets Fund was priced at $10 a share on the original offering. However, the early trading encouraged the price to shoot up to $15. The fund raised $100 million and will invest at least 75 percent of its resources in companies in "emerging" areas of the world. Of the 95 Third World countries, 42 have been qualified as secure enough by the fund management to receive some of the investments.

I believe that this fund will appeal to Americans who want to help the disadvantaged in poor countries, but want to do it through job creation rather than charity. In effect, I believe that it is possible for one to do "well" at the same time that one is doing "good."

During a ten-year period which ended in 1984, the emerging countries experienced an average growth rate of about 5 percent compared to an average rate of 2.4 percent for industrialized countries. Now, the

Templeton Fund plans to invest in 42 emerging countries from Argentina to Zimbabwe. Some have securities markets to which foreign investors have some access. Currently, over 6,000 securities are listed on such emerging country securities markets, with a total market capitalization of over $150 billion. By way of comparison, over 15,000 securities are listed on industrialized country securities markets, with a total market capitalization of about $6 trillion. The Templeton Fund hopes to purchase and hold securities for long-term capital appreciation and to maintain an annual portfolio turnover rate of under 50 percent.

The Templeton Fund is just the beginning of what could become an important trend in supplying capital to financially starved countries. Although $100 million is but a drop in the bucket as far as their needs are concerned, every little bit will help. We will have to go a long way to match the $25 to $35 billion amounts which were lent annually to the Third World during the late 1970s, but already, there is a second fund, appropriately called the Discovery Fund, which will partially invest in Third World countries. The Price group is currently offering shares in this closed-end fund. If the public gobbles up these shares, more funds will surely follow.

It is interesting to note that the Taiwanese and Korean funds sell at the biggest premiums among closed-end foreign country funds. Premiums paid by investors for Third World funds suggests that the demand for developing country equity products exceeds the supply. Therefore, such countries should encourage private companies to go public by better tax treatment of dividends and capital gains; privatize their nationalized industries; bolster stock trading by instituting better regulation and more reliable accounting standards; relax restrictions on foreign investments in domestic companies; and allow the full repatriation of dividends.

In one recent year, $34 billion in economic aid and $25 billion in bank loans were transferred to poor countries. However, most of these funds went to governments for huge infrastructure projects and inefficient government corporations. What a waste! Last year, Mexico alone closed 44 of these unprofitable state-owned corporations.

What is needed are equity investments and business loans in small- to medium-sized enterprises. Citizens in many countries are a step ahead of their governments, having established free markets in the informal economy. For example, in the Dominican Republic the Association for the Development of Microbusiness has done wonders with a small-stake loan program involving only $330,000.

The mutual fund format can become an important provider of capital in poor countries which would permit the privatization of many enterprises. Also the mutual fund format is a very efficient, low-cost intermediary for fostering democratic people's capitalism. Already Americans have invested $50 billion in shares of foreign enterprises. Wouldn't it be great if one or two billion dollars were to "trickle down" to the poorest countries?

China

At the beginning of 1986, *Time* magazine featured a picture of Deng Xiaoping on its cover as its "Man of the Year." The reason: he is moving China toward a more market-oriented approach. The Chinese government is permitting a little enterprise to develop, but it doesn't want such reform to change the existing political system. Therefore, allowed enterprises are limited to family businesses. The government is afraid to encourage the formation of real corporations.

But China needs billions in capital to modernize and catch up with the rest of the world. Practical Chinese officials know that stock and bond markets are necessary if they are to raise the needed capital. Therefore, it is not surprising that rudimentary stock exchanges are beginning to operate in Bejing and in Shanghai. Of course, there are restrictions: stock can be sold in government enterprises, but only to workers. (Isn't it ironic that in the workers' paradise there is a need for the "owners of the means of production" to actually own some common stock in their enterprises in order to give them the proper incentives?)

However, the Chinese are planning to make a real public offering of some shares. A Chinese company will be the first to be publicly traded on an international stock exchange, through a listing in Hong Kong in 1987. Public trading in this provincial government enterprise in southern China would mark the first time since the communists came to power in 1949 that a Chinese company has turned to a foreign stock market to raise capital. The implication for the world-wide privatization movement is enormous.

The Soviet Union

While the whole world is moving away from central control of the economy and toward freedom and private ownership, Russia is locked into an obsolete system which is having increasing trouble just producing the wealth it needs to maintain its military machine. It is nowhere near the third wave status of the United States, being so heavily dependent upon the old technologies emblazoned on its logo—the hammer of the second wave and the sickle of the first.

The Soviets suffer from centralized planning and centralized command. All information and communication is controlled by the state. Even photocopy machines are strictly controlled. No computers, not even word processors, are privately owned. Soviet managers have no incentive to overproduce to increase productivity.

The paradox of the Soviet Union is that while their military is modern and strong, their internal economy is weak and they are falling further behind the United States. With the opening up of some controlled criticism together with the possibility of an arms control agreement in the offing, Gorbachev may be able to buy the time he needs to figure out how to get the economy off dead center, but the outlook for the U.S.S.R. is grim indeed.

Conclusion

Natural trends in a variety of countries are moving steadily toward capitalism and free enterprise. Socialism is not gaining ground as a viable economic alternative, no matter what its other attractions might be, in regions where it was once a welcome and preferred economic strategy. But while the rest of the world is learning the benefits of capitalism, we in the United States seem to be adopting anti-capitalistic measures that could hamstring our economy. Significantly, we are on the verge of repeating the mistakes of the early 1930s with our current flirtation with tariff measures against nations that are giving us good quality products at low prices, and there are other alarming portents as well. The new tax law is beneficial to our economy. The action of our stock market since the beginning of this year attests to that. However, the new law is very unfriendly toward capital which is now taxed at a marginal rate (28 percent) which is much higher than last year (20 percent). This is not just an 8 percent increase; it is a 40 percent increase (8 over 20).

Another problem we have is our "socialistic" instincts, best described by Austrian economist, Friedrich von Hayek. Our instincts, he tells us, encourage us to serve the known needs of known people. However, we can do more good to unknown people if we follow the impersonal signals of the market. Whereas the Soviet Union encourages the spread of communism throughout the world by aiding political parties and front movements, the United States does little to encourage the investment of risk capital that could do much to improve the condition of people everywhere. It is to be hoped that the powerful engines of change articulated by earlier champions of the free market— through the "invisible hand" of Adam Smith and David Ricardo's wealth-building comparative advantages from voluntary trade—are stronger than all the efforts of governments to try to stop them.

The positive effects of capitalism, privatization, foreign trade and investment are also a powerful force in the dissemination of the worth of the individual and democratic ideas in general. Ludwig von Mises explained long ago why it is impossible to allocate resources rationally in planned economic systems: they lack the information base provided by the price system to allocate resources efficiently. The price system does a better job because it is based on free trade and private ownership.

Capitalism is on the move. We ought to understand the dynamic changes which are going our way, and give them a boost. More than our economic well-being is at stake. The interdependence created by trade and investment are a more powerful force for the mainte-nance of peace than all the anti-nuclear demonstrations and all the treaties we could possibly sign. In this lies the best news of all, and it is news we should spread.

Arthur Shenfield

In the Socialist Camp

My first task here is to define or delimit the socialist camp. What countries come within its ambit? Clearly it is arguable that large parts of what is called the "free world" might also be logically included in the socialist camp, at least within the context of privatization. Thus Britain, France and Italy are obvious examples of countries where much enterprise was nationalized or socialized in the 20th century under the avowed influence of socialist ideologies (including, in the Italian case, fascism, which, contrary to widespread misunderstanding, is a branch of socialism). In Britain and France the current drive towards privatization or denationalization is a product of a conscious revulsion with the policies and influence of previous socialist governments. Ideas strongly infused with socialist thinking are evident in examples of U.S. public ownership, such as the Tennessee Valley Authority, Amtrak and Conrail, even though the great majority of Americans would not perceive this to be so.

I will also restrict my attention to the obvious examples in the socialist camp—the Soviet Union, its European satellites as well as Yugoslavia, mainland China, and those parts of the Third World (accounting for much of it) where those in power either have consciously rejected the free-market or capitalistic economy, or have established pervasive state ownership, direction or control simply because they are despots who are doing what comes naturally.

But why privatization in the socialist camp? By definition, isn't privatization incompatible with socialist principles? The answer is that in the socialist world, in degrees varying substantially from country to country, a movement has arisen to loosen the economic grip of the state. It may be that some rulers have come to the conclusion that full-blooded socialism does not work, or that socialism is improved and made more efficient if mixed with a small dose of capitalism; or it may merely be evidence of a tactical decision to *reculer pour mieux sauter*, i.e., to take one step back from socialism in order to take two steps forward later. In practice all three of these motivations are discernible, though it is quite possible that the most powerful one of all will turn out to be the recognition that full-blooded socialism simply does not work. If this is the case, we may be witnessing the beginnings of a splendid change in the winds which blow upon the mind of mankind. From the recognition that full-blooded socialism does not work, it is not a distant step to the truth: no socialism works. If, then, progress to society's basics of liberty and private property is slow and halting, it will not be because men remain hooked on socialist ideology, but because the victory of the general interest over the sectional interests (which socialism invariably produces) also involves a hard and slow grind.

The Soviet Union

Let us first consider the inner citadel of socialism. The Soviet Union, from 1917 to 1921, had nothing, at least superficially, that could truly be called a system. Later one developed under the auspices of the Five-Year Plans, Gosplan and Gosbank, but what Lenin and Trotsky presided over until 1921 was chaos in its crudest sense. Stalin's relentless drive to socialize agriculture in the 1930s led to the deaths of millions because that was both implicit and explicit in the plan, but from 1917 to 1921 millions died simply because of chaos. The reason was that Lenin and Trotsky had swallowed a basic Marxist notion of staggering naïveté, namely that every economic system is simply an emanation of the class ownership of the means of production. Hence, if one wished to produce a socialist economy from the womb of capitalism, one had only to remove the capitalist owners of the means of production. That was why in all his turgid advocacy of socialism Marx never seriously bothered to consider how a socialist economy would work. It would work, he supposed, because the ownership of the means of production would be socialized.

So Lenin and Trotsky executed or expropriated hundreds of thousands of those whom they designated as capitalists or landowners, and then confidently expected a splendidly workable socialist system to arise Phoenix-like without a plan or organization or coordination. Socialist production and distribution would simply arise in perfect form because ownership had become social instead of private. Of course, they quickly found that there had to be some organization or direction to get anything at all from A to B, from producer to consumer. But at that time everything was done ad hoc, the product of improvisation, while all failures, which were many, were held to be the result of sabotage, punishable by death.

In 1921 Lenin proclaimed his NEP, or New Economic Policy. Nowadays many would hail it as a move towards privatization. In fact it was truly a case of *reculer pour mieux sauter.* Lenin did not believe in the superior efficiency of private enterprise, nor did he understand the workings of private market activity. His NEP provided some temporary private control, though less than true private ownership, simply because he did not know how to deal with the mounting

and pressing problems arising from the chaos which
he and Trotsky had produced. His fatuous slogan
"Soviet power plus electrification makes socialism" in-
dicates the extreme paucity of his understanding. In
practice all his NEP amounted to was a temporary
freedom for the peasants to sell their surplus food-
stuffs privately. In industry it was mainly a sham.

In 1924 Lenin died. Stalin took over and Trotsky
fled, ultimately to be assassinated by Stalin's agent. In
the 1930s Stalin imposed the collectivization of agriculture, which Lenin and Trotsky had never got round
to, incurring an immense cost in lives by deliberate and
sweeping policies of starvation and execution. This
calumny aside, Stalin's strategy had other consequences, too; it caused major inefficiency in Russian
food production which has persisted to this day. So
disastrous were the results that Stalin was obliged after
a time to allow the peasants to farm small plots of land,
set apart from the large collective farms, mainly for the
production of vegetables and fruits for private sale.
This was something like a partial reversion to Lenin's
NEP. Though the first measure of freedom thus
allowed was minute, in due time these plots, amount-
ing to no more than about 3 percent of the country's
cultivated land, have accounted for as much as 30
percent of total food production. Remarkable as it may
seem, the Soviet Union has for several decades presented an example of highly beneficial privatization.

Soviet industry has continued to operate largely under the benighted inefficiency of governmental ownership and centralized economic planning. The results are familiar—shoddy workmanship and huge shortages—but with two notable qualifications. First, though it is clear that the production of civilian goods is hopelessly inefficient, it is generally accepted in the West that in the field of military goods the results are quite different. When it comes to guns, tanks, missiles and the rest, Soviet production is both high-quality and ample, indeed too ample for our comfort. However, it is doubtful whether most Western observers can verify this assumption. Certainly the Pentagon manages to obtain a supply of Russian military products to test their capabilities, but their evaluations are classified. The only evidence available to the public comes from actual combat. Combat in, for example, the Israeli-Syrian confrontations suggests that perhaps some Russian products are inferior to those of the West, though the more obvious problems appear to include differences in military skills and other human qualities. Doubtless, it is caution which justifies an assumption that the quality of Russian military products merits respect, despite the strong theoretical presumption that *all* production in a centrally planned economy is likely to be inefficient.

The second qualification arises from the fact that private enterprise of a certain kind does keep the wheels of Soviet industry going round. Though illegal and punishable by severe penalties, including death, enterprising unofficial middlemen make profits by nosing out shortages and misplaced surpluses, of which there are many, and bringing them into some rough kind of marriage. Of course the middleman cannot be as successful as his talents would allow him to be in a free economy, because he must not allow his operations to become too obvious. The government's planners in all likelihood keep a close surveillance over his operations, which help them to correct their own manifold errors and prop up a failing economy. His actions are welcome only so long as they are conducted quietly—lest they disturb the official presumption that the planners know what they are doing.

But now Mr. Gorbachev has stepped onto the stage. His innovations, whether genuine or a mere ploy to serve him in his *pas de deux* with the West, are primarily concerned with noneconomic matters. However, he has let a faint breath of fresh air into the Soviet economy by allowing some degree of private enterprise in such services as taxi driving, shoe repair, home plumbing, and small-scale construction. Insofar as these changes are genuine, they are a case of privatization designed to alleviate the acute shortages and delays which plague the Russian consumer.

But are they genuine? If so, can they last? If they last, are they the beginnings of a true liberalization of the Soviet economy? From such acorns great oaks may grow. All we can say is that resistance to such liberalization is sure to be powerful. It is not simply a case of natural inertia. The great resistance will come from the upper echelons of the Russian class society whose privileges are entrenched. For the favored few, the Soviet system is a good society, as good as or better than that enjoyed by any feudal lord of yore. What happens to the millions of unfortunate "proles" beneath them as a result of the desperate inefficiencies of the collectivized planned economy leaves their withers quite unwrung. The outlook for the liberalization of the Soviet economy is therefore uncertain. But let us take comfort from this fact. However faint the wind may be, if it blows at all, it blows, even in the Soviet Union, in the direction of liberty. And in some other parts of the socialist camp where it has begun to blow, it is with no mean force.

The Soviet Union's European Satellites

The showpiece of privatization among the Soviet Union's European satellites is Hungary. In 1956 Russian tanks rolled into Budapest and suppressed the people's uprising against communist tyranny with barbaric cruelty. Janos Kadar, who had betrayed his leader, Imre Nagy, to the Soviet overlords, was installed as a puppet ruler. For some twelve years, Hungary displayed a picture of a nation almost sleep-walking in subjection. But the qualities that had distinguished the

Magyars for nearly a thousand years among European peoples—dash, bravura, flamboyance—had been stilled, but not eradicated. From about 1968 they reemerged to create what has become known popularly as "goulash communism," a center of economic innovation in the communist world presided over, surprisingly, by that same Janos Kadar, the obedient Soviet puppet.

In Hungary, plumbers, electricians, taxi drivers, restaurateurs and shopkeepers ply their trades for private gain as independent entrepreneurs. The Hungarian standard of living is distinctly higher than that of all other Soviet European satellites except East Germany, which inevitably benefits from the proximity of highly prosperous West Germany. It is estimated that some five million East Europeans come to Hungary annually for the shopping. Western visitors to Budapest nowadays report that it looks more like a Western free city than other drab, depressing communist capitals. About 40 percent of the food supply is produced by private farmers who are essentially free. Perhaps most important of all, in principle though not yet in practice, is the fact that Hungarians may bid for unsuccessful state-owned enterprises and operate them during limited periods for a percentage of the surpluses (which are not yet officially called profits).

How is it that Moscow tolerates the existence of this communist anomaly? There are two main reasons. Firstly, Janos Kadar has demonstrated to the Moscow overlords that he is their most faithful and subservient ally in all international affairs. For this they consider dabbling in free-market activity a reasonable price to pay. Secondly, it remains the case that over 90 percent of Hungarian industrial output still comes from state-owned enterprises, and the great part of foreign trade is with other Soviet bloc countries. Thus the Soviet leaders are satisfied that the Hungarian economy essentially adheres to the communist model. But are they right?

No one needs to be told that Poland is the most awkward subject among the European satellites. In population it is by far the largest. Its virile hatred and contempt for the Russians dates back at least two centuries when Russia gained control over the largest and most central segment of the country. Its vigorous and deep-rooted Catholic faith not only differentiates it from its Russian overlord, but also preserves and reinforces the national spirit.

Poland's standard of living has long been higher than Russia's. In Czarist days, Warsaw and Lodz were the most industrialized cities in the Russian Empire. Since their post-World War II subjugation by the Soviets, the Poles have continued on average to live better than the Russian proletariat, mainly because Polish agriculture was not collectivized along the lines of the Russian model. Eighty percent of Poland's farmland is in private hands, which is the main reason why, unlike other satellites, Poland has been a significant exporter of foods, especially pork and ham, to Western countries. Of course the Polish farmers are by no means free entrepreneurs. They are regulated, controlled and pushed around by the government's planners. Most telling is that prices for domestic consumption goods are determined wholly by the government. Yet such is the difference between private and collectivized ownership that, even with the heavy hand of the state upon them, the Polish farmers have sufficient incentive to put some heart into what they do.

Over the last few years, however, the Polish economy has deteriorated. Government regulation in both agriculture and industry has become more stringent, partly as a reaction to the Solidarity movement and the threat it poses to the government's tyranny. No longer do the Polish farmers export any significant amount of food to the West, and the supply of manufactures to the consumer is conspicuously less satisfactory than it was only a decade ago.

These conditions and the itch for freedom, which after all is irrepressible in the human breast, have forced the authorities to take a new look at their economic programs. Faced with economic stagnation, and perhaps encouraged by Gorbachev's apparent but not yet confirmed endorsement, the Polish government is, as of this writing, considering some radical economic reforms. The reform plan, which would introduce a striking measure of privatization into the economy, is sure to meet powerful opposition from entrenched *apparatchiks.* But government officials have themselves said that the plan, if fulfilled, would rank Poland with Hungary and China, among the most progressive in revising traditional communist economic policies and practices. In addition to easing the hand of government over the farmers, and to giving permission for a good deal of private enterprise in services per the Hungarian model, the plan would create in industry some mixed capital ventures involving shared ownership between the state and private investors. Stanislaw Kwiatkowski, a close adviser to General Jaruzelski, has been quoted in the journal *Polityka* as saying that "the invigoration of the economy should be based on a diversity of forms of ownership of the means of production" (what heresy for a Marxist!), and that "if high-earning employees could spend part of their incomes on the purchase of stocks and bonds, the effect could be truly motivational" (sounding almost like Mrs. Thatcher!).

One reason why some members of the Polish government hope that the reform plan will go into effect is that they intend to apply to the International Monetary Fund for a standby loan. If that succeeds, they hope to obtain credits from Western banks and governments, such as have not been forthcoming since 1981.

Of the other Soviet European satellites there is little new to report. East Germany is the most successful, or rather the least unsuccessful, of their economies, part-

ly because the German will to work has not been de-
stroyed by regimentation, but mainly because the
availability of consumer and capital goods is boosted
by trade with highly successful West Germany. Black-
mail is also an important element: For example, old
people in the East are allowed to move to the West on
terms very advantageous to the East German government. But as yet, there is no sign of any significant
move towards privatization in the economy.

The Czechs, and perhaps the Slovaks, have a higher
standard of living than the Russians. As in Poland,
their agriculture has not been collectivized, though of
course it is regimented. The Czechs have a longer
history and experience of industry, with its concom-
itant skills, than any other of the satellite peoples except the East Germans. But in character they are a
conformist, nonrebellious people (even under their
great leader, Masaryk, they did not aim at secession
from the Hapsburg Empire until late in World War I
when it became clear that Austria-Hungary was on the
losing side), and as yet they are displaying no tendency
to follow the Hungarian and the incipient Polish line.
The Slovaks have no fond memories of the Magyars,
while neither they nor the Czechs care much for the
Poles. The wind of change will have to blow a good
deal stronger if we are to see some liberation in the
Czechoslovakian economy. They have no urge as yet to
attempt a repetition even of the mild Dubchek reforms
which the Russians heavy-handedly put down in 1968.

Rumania is a maverick among the satellites. On the one hand, it is the least subservient to the Russians in international affairs—for example, going its own way in relations with Israel and even to some extent with the West. On the other hand, its economy is the most regimented and irrationally managed of them all. However, Rumania's economic tyranny is not really a reflection of communist or Marxist theory or practice. The fact is that Mr. Ceausescu, the Rumanian dictator, is a political boss who treats his country as a private fief which exists for the benefit of himself, his family and his numerous relatives and cronies. He is a quasi-communist version of Somoza, Stroessner, Marcos, and Papa Doc and Baby Doc Duvalier, but worse than any of them. Ceausescu's death, or downfall, if either should occur, may herald some genuine liberation for the Rumanian people insofar as Moscow allows it, or Rumania might well follow the familiar pattern of one boss being succeeded by another.

Of Bulgaria we need only say that it is the most loyal and subservient of all the Soviet satellites, and will make no change that does not receive the approval of Moscow. So far it has not even dared to follow in the footsteps of Gorbachev. Nor will it do so until it becomes clear that the path is safe to tread.

Yugoslavia

Yugoslavia is not a Soviet satellite. It is now nearly forty years since Tito rebelled against Soviet hegemony. Furthermore, Yugoslavia not only broke away from the Marxist heartland, it also began to introduce what appeared to be a substantial element of market force into its economy. Principally, it reorganized factories and other workplaces to allow their workers to earn profits and compete with each other. In the 1960s, and increasingly in the 1970s, this system appeared to be successful, and Western observers flocked to Yugoslavia to see how this form of privatization, an apparent halfway house between a socialist and a free economy, worked. There is no doubt that this system lifted the Yugoslav economy above the levels of the Soviet Union and its satellites. Even though Yugoslavia was basically a poor country and, outside Slovenia and Croatia, a primitive one by Western European standards, its economy was clearly more open than those of other bloc countries and, equally clearly, delivered on average a better standard of living than they did. Essentially the Yugoslav economy was an example of market or semimarket syndicalism which, though much inferior to full-fledged free enterprise, was superior to centrally planned collectivism.

Since Tito's death in 1981 the Yugoslav economy has deteriorated. It no longer attracts the interest of Western observers, and in general it now presents a picture of considerable disarray. Does this mean that it is an example of the failure of privatization? In the main the answer is that market or semimarket syndicalism is not a satisfactory form of privatization, though it may produce fair results for a time and up to a point. Its essential defect is that in the absence of individual freedom in the disposition of resources, it cannot produce an efficient market for capital. The control of the supply of capital remains mainly in bureaucratic hands, while even that part of capital supply generated within each syndicalist unit has no true bench mark to indicate its economic value and the return which it should generate. In short, successful privatization must move resources—above all, capital—to a true private market.

There is another important element in the Yugoslav story. Yugoslavia is an exceptionally difficult country to govern. It is composed of several different nationalities with different histories and characters. The Serbs are the largest and hence politically dominant, but they are despised by the Slovenes and Croats. The Slovenes and Croats are Catholics and use the Latin script; the Serbs are Greek Orthodox and use the Cyrillic script. In Hapsburg days the Slovenes lived in relatively liberal and advanced Austria. The Croats lived in less liberal, but almost as advanced Hungary and were protected by the Hapsburgs from excessive Magyar domination. The Serbs lived for four centuries under benighted Turkish rule and, in Slovene and Croat eyes, came to independence as a mere pack of ignorant peasants. Other smaller groups with distinct histories also exist, e.g., the Montenegrins and the Bosnians. No other European country has so much difficult diversity within itself. Though a Croat, Tito controlled the Serbs and with a firm hand held the country together. That his successors have found the task more difficult has had demonstrable effects upon the performance of the economy.

What of the future? It may be that Yugoslavia will continue to putter along as a sick man of Europe, perhaps until a new strong man arises to take grip of its situation. Will he move the country back to the benighted, centralized, collectivized pattern, or forward to some measure of true liberalization? It is my guess that with the wind of change now blowing in at least some parts of Eastern Europe, it is more likely to be forward than backward.

China

China presents the most important example of privatization in the socialist world. She accounts for more than one-fifth of all the human beings on our planet. She may possibly be on the way to a larger measure of privatization than any other country in the socialist camp. Furthermore, if her privatization does proceed as some predict, the effect could be the world's most significant recoil from all-pervasive socialism. For in some ways Mao Tse-tung pushed the Chinese deeper into the socialist morass than Lenin, Trotsky, or even Stalin pushed the Russians. There is little doubt that in sheer numbers Mao was responsible for the deaths of more people than Stalin or Hitler, a feat uncompromised by the fact that these deaths represented a smaller percentage of the total population.

More recently, under Deng Xiaoping the Chinese consumer, like his counterpart in Hungary, has been allowed the benefit of more and more private enterprise in services. But not only in services. Whereas not long ago material aspirations for millions of Chinese were fulfilled by the possession of a bicycle, a wrist watch and, for women, a foot-powered sewing machine, now they can hope for a color-television set, a refrigerator, and even a cassette player (an automobile, though, is still a far-off dream). Furthermore, increasing numbers of Western businessmen and tourists are being encouraged to come to China, and the services which they require, notably modern hotels that suit Western expectations, are being assiduously developed. At the same time thousands of students are being sent abroad to learn how Westerners live and work. Already Shanghai, a ghost city in Mao's time, is beginning to look something like the citadel of capitalism it was in pre-communist days. In October 1984 the Central Committee of the Chinese Communist Party actually stated that "Only when some individuals are allowed and encouraged to get better off [sic] by diligent work, will more and more people be prompted to take the road to prosperity." In order to raise funds, some state-owned enterprises have actually been authorized to issue bonds and the equivalent of stocks with dividends becoming payable to worker-stockholders, though admittedly this development has not yet gotten far off the ground.

Since Deng came into effective power nearly nine years ago, many rural communes—the most un-Chinese phenomenon in 3,000 years or more—have been abolished and family farms restored. In industry, managers have been authorized to institute bonus-pay schemes in order to reward superior workers and to differentiate them from inferior ones. Consequently, there has been a distinct rise in the incomes of peasants, still by far the majority of the Chinese people, and of workers in manufacturing and service industries.

We should not be surprised to find, however, that not all is smooth sailing on this route. In January 1987 Hu Yaobang, who was the titular head of the Chinese Communist Party and the most forceful proponent of these changes, was forced to resign. The majority on the Politburo thought that the changes were proceeding too fast and too far, and Deng himself thought that they were stirring expectations which could threaten the existence of the Party itself. What gave Deng pause, and perhaps frightened him, was the sight of recent student demonstrations and protests, just as if China had become a free Western-style country. Thus the conservative elements in the Party have regained influence. But such was inevitable. Changes of this

character cannot proceed in a straight line, ever on-
ward and upward. For any totalitarian or authori-
tarian government, they present a difficult and anxious
situation. The rulers see the benefits of liberalization
and privatization, but they also see that those benefits
must bring a reduction in their own power. "Where,"
they ask themselves, "will it stop? Will it actually lead to
democracy, so that we shall some day have to submit to
free elections?" This presents them with an agonizing
dilemma. At some stages they will surely halt and
attempt to backtrack. Yet the logic of reform is in-
escapable. Once it has gained a fair impetus, the people will inevitably demand more of it, and the rulers
will find that they are powerless to go back to the
starting point. Brutal repression becomes impracti-
cable when people have acquired a taste for freedom.

Earlier the question was posed whether the Soviet
rulers are justified in their contentment with Hungary—that its economy essentially adheres to the communist model. If they are right, it can only be because
the liberalization of the Hungarian economy has not
yet reached a critical point. If it has reached that point,
as may well be the case, the Soviets will rue the day
when they allowed the Hungarians to go as far as they
have.

In the case of China I believe that the die is cast—the
liberalization movement is now irreversible. If the internal evidence is not yet sufficient to justify my opti-
mism, I believe that the following does. In 1997 Hong

Kong will be ceded to China, and now the Portuguese have agreed to cede Macao shortly thereafter. The Bejing government has formally agreed with the British government that for at least 50 years after the cession the people of Hong Kong will be allowed to retain a free-market economy. If Bejing keeps its word, the prosperity and liberty of Hong Kong, which by then will be an integral part of China, will have lighted a candle for the mainland people which will be extremely difficult, if at all possible, to extinguish. At the same time the flow of foreign currency which already finds its way to mainland China through Hong Kong will increase, making the maintenance of Hong Kong's freedom of enterprise all the more attractive. The accession of little Macao, with its revenue-producing casino and the gamblers attracted by it, must surely reinforce pro-market sentiment. The pressure for further liberalization on the mainland will surely take it beyond the critical point, if it has not reached it already. If, on the other hand, Bejing breaks its word, solemnly given to the British government and thereby to Hong Kong's citizenry, it will not only suffer heavy material loss; it will unleash a wave of reaction around the world which can only bring harm to itself.

The Third World

A lengthy disquisition on privatization in the Third World is not called for here. Its member countries all have mixed economies with varying proportions of state-owned enterprise and that which is privately held. A major problem is that Third World private enterprise is often effectively made public by witless or corrupt governmental intervention. Some countries, like Brazil, Argentina and Mexico, enjoy a considerable amount of private enterprise and a goodly supply of competent private entrepreneurs. If they were to put their fiscal houses in order, these countries could graduate from the Third World column with enormous benefit and without unbearable pain. Of course, this is politically difficult, which is why it is not done. But with limited temporary help from the developed countries, it could be accomplished (barring the not uncommon fact that help is sometimes immediately swallowed up by fiscal extravagance). The World Bank, the IMF, and the U.S. Agency for International Development (AID), among others, have made this point clear, so the problem essentially appears to be one of political will.

Other Third World countries, typically those in Africa, also have mixed economies, but their maladies arise from the fact that they tend to have corrupt, tyrannical, sometimes even murderous governments. They do not have true socialist or communist infrastructures, although in some cases their rulers represent them as such. Private enterprise cannot thrive in such a climate, but at least the cause and the remedy are clear. The cause is international aid, principally from the United States but also from Western European countries. The aid curseth him that gives and him that takes, especially the latter. It makes government the source of all material advancement, and thus extinguishes incentives to prosper by private business activity. It burns the roots of private capital markets, if they exist at all, and makes all significant development a government prerogative, which too often means capital waste and nondevelopment. The first step in the remedy is the termination of government-to-government aid. Thereafter, steps must be taken to promote regimes which will be attractive to private capital and enterprise, largely from the developed world but also the indigenous, and which will maintain a framework of law that will enable private capital and enterprise to flourish.

Conclusion

At the outset, I ventured to observe that we may be witnessing the beginnings of a splendid change in the winds which blow upon the mind of mankind. The evidence adduced about the development of privatization is of mixed character, but I believe that it may well confirm this happy possibility. From the developed world to the industrial world, from the democratic camp to the socialist camp, the merits of free human action are obvious. Let us hope that they are allowed to increase and prosper.